# The Case
## of the
# Mystery Mark

Other Middle Grade Books by
## ANGELA ELWELL HUNT

### THE NICKI HOLLAND MYSTERY SERIES

*The Case of the Mystery Mark*
*The Case of the Phantom Friend*
*The Case of the Teenage Terminator*
*The Case of the Terrified Track Star*
*The Case of the Counterfeit Cash*

*The Case of the Haunting*
*of Lowell Lanes*
*The Case of the Birthday Bracelet*
*The Secret of Cravenhill Castle*
*The Riddle of Baby Rosalind*

### THE CASSIE PERKINS SERIES

*No More Broken Promises*
*A Forever Friend*
*A Basket of Roses*
*A Dream to Cherish*
*The Much-Adored Sandy Shore*

*Love Burning Bright*
*Star Light, Star Bright*
*The Chance of a Lifetime*
*The Glory of Love*

### THE YOUNG BELIEVERS SERIES,
### with Steve Arterburn

*Josiah*
*Liane*
*Taz*

*Shane*
*Paige*
*Noah*

### THE COLONIAL CAPTIVES SERIES

*Kimberly and the Captives*

*The Deadly Chase*

ii

NICKI HOLLAND MYSTERIES

# The Case
# of the
# Mystery Mark

### Angela Elwell Hunt

**Tommy nelson**™
For Tweens and Teens

A Division of Thomas Nelson Publishers
Since 1798

www.thomasnelson.com

THE CASE OF THE MYSTERY MARK
Copyright © 1991 by Angela Elwell Hunt

Published in Nashville, Tennessee, by Tommy Nelson®, a Division of Thomas Nelson, Inc. Visit us on the Web at www.tommynelson.com.

Scripture quotations are from the *International Children's Bible*®, *New Century Version*®, copyright © 1986, 1988, 1999 by Tommy Nelson®, a Division of Thomas Nelson, Inc.

Tommy Nelson® books may be purchased in bulk for educational, business, fund-raising, or sales promotional use. For information, please e-mail us at SpecialMarkets@ThomasNelson.com.

This is a work of fiction. Names, characters, places, and incidents either are the product of the author's imagination or are used fictitiously.

Interior: Jennifer Ross / MJ Ross Design

ISBN 1-4003-0763-5

Printed in the United States of America
05 06 07 08 09 WRZ 9 8 7 6 5 4 3 2 1

# One

Riding to school with Laura Cushman in a chauffeur-driven Rolls-Royce, Nicki Holland leaned back into the leather upholstery and thought her seventh-grade year was certainly starting out right. With a new haircut, new clothes, and a new friend, nothing could go wrong. Absolutely nothing.

Last year she had walked to school every day with her best friends Christine Kelshaw and Meredith Dixon, but since meeting Laura two months ago, Nicki's life had been spent in luxury. At least when she was with Laura, that is. When she was at home, life was pretty much ho-hum normal.

Nicki could see Christine and Meredith up ahead, walking together. "Hey, Laura, can't we stop and pick them up? They'd love it!"

Laura looked a little doubtful, but she tapped on the glass separating the driver from his passengers and pointed to the curb. He smoothly pulled over until the sleek car was alongside the startled girls.

Nicki lowered her window. "Hey, Christine! Meredith! Want to ride to school in style?"

Meredith dropped her jaw. "Is that you, Nicki?"

Christine giggled, but she hesitated only a minute. "Sure, we'll ride." They piled in.

Christine looked at Nicki as the car pulled into traffic. "We wondered where you'd been all summer."

"I'm sorry I haven't been around much," Nicki said. "But after I met Laura we spent a week on the beach, and then a week at Disney World with her mother. Last week we were so busy shopping for school clothes I didn't have a chance to call either of you."

"That's okay, Nick, we forgive you." Meredith sniffed, pretending to be upset. She wound a curl of her long, dark hair around her finger and smiled at Laura. "Even though our best friend has ignored us since you came along, it's nice to meet you. I'm Meredith Dixon—"

"The brain," interrupted Christine. "And I'm Christine Kelshaw of the famous Kelshaw clan."

"She says that because she has five brothers and sisters," Nicki explained. "And they're all redheads like Chris. If you ever want peace and quiet, *don't* go to Christine's house."

Meredith's eyes were bugging as she looked around. "Is this your car?"

Laura gave her a little smile. "It's my mother's."

Meredith and Christine looked at Nicki. "Moving up in the world, huh?"

"Laura and I met at the mall," Nicki explained. "She was new and didn't know where anything was, so I helped her find Burdines." She rolled her eyes. "You haven't gone shopping until you've gone to the mall with Laura."

"I can imagine," Meredith said. "What are you, a model or something?"

Laura blushed and shook her head.

"She could be," Nicki said, sensing Laura's embarrassment. Even at twelve, Laura was so pretty that grown men stopped and stared at her. Nicki couldn't help feeling like an ugly duckling when she was with Laura, but sometimes she felt sorry for the girl. She seemed so alone.

"Why don't you go to Beachcrest Prep?" Christine asked. "That's where the other rich kids go."

"I wanted to go where Nicki goes to school," Laura answered, her face stiff. "She's my only friend in Pine Grove."

Christine nodded. "Oh."

"That's some accent," Meredith said. "Where are you from?"

"Georgia." Laura blushed again.

"I liked her southern accent," Nicki said. Really, everything sounded dignified when Laura said it. *Ah'd like shrimp, puh-leese. Ah like the peach color bet-tuh.* But now Laura was quieter than Nicki had ever seen her.

The girls settled back and rode in silence. Nicki felt uneasy for Laura—being new was hard enough, being megarich would make things harder. Nicki knew the car alone was enough to drop jaws all over the campus of Pine Grove Middle School. Laura was going to need help, but Meredith and Christine were Nicki's best friends and she didn't want to sacrifice their friendship to help Laura feel secure.

"You guys, I just know this is going to be a great year," Nicki said. "Together we four are going to be the best of friends.

We'll be in homeroom together, take classes together, and no one will be able to tear us apart. Okay?"

Christine flashed a grin and Meredith nodded, but Laura's brows lowered. "Are you sure?"

"If Nicki says you're okay, then you're okay with us," Christine said cheerfully, snapping her gum. "But I really think you should tell your mother to forget the limo. Once is pretty cool, but any more than that . . . well, people will think you're showing off."

Laura looked puzzled. "Then how will I get to school? I live out in Gatscomb Hills and it's too far to walk. Mother would die before she'd let me ride a bus."

"That's what you get for living out in the Hills," Christine said. "Most of the kids in school live either in our subdivision or in Levitt Park Apartments."

"I have an idea," Nicki said, feeling her shoulder-length brown hair swish over her arms just as Laura's hair stylist said it would. "Just have the driver drop you at my house. Then we can all walk to school together."

"What if it rains?"

Christine laughed. "Then tell your mom to have you delivered in something a little more ordinary. A Rolls-Royce isn't going to help you fit in around here."

"More ordinary—like a Mercedes?"

Christine sighed. "Like a Ford."

—

Nicki, Meredith, and Christine had Mrs. Balian for English in sixth grade, so Nicki was pleasantly surprised to learn that Mrs. Balian was in charge of their seventh-grade homeroom. It was nice to walk into school on the first day of a new year and have a teacher who already knew your name.

Last year a rumor about Mrs. Balian had floated around school—some kids said she had been first runner-up in the Miss America Pageant, but no one had the nerve to ask her if it was true. How would you ask such a question? If you acted like you thought it was true and it wasn't, she'd think you were stupid for believing such a wild story. If you acted like you thought it wasn't true and it was, she'd be insulted that you didn't think she was Miss America material. So no one asked and no one knew for sure. Nicki figured that's why rumors stayed rumors instead of becoming proven fact.

Mrs. Balian didn't care where anyone sat in homeroom. Meredith, Laura, Christine, and Nicki sat in desks opposite the door so they could see everyone coming in. After a long summer, it was good to see who was back and who had changed.

Scott Spence, tall and good-looking, was back and much improved over last year's sixth-grade edition. "I think he's grown six inches in three months," Christine said, giggling.

"I'd say five and three-quarter inches," Meredith deduced, peering at him through her clear slide rule.

Nicki perked up. Last year she had the unfortunate distinction of being the tallest girl in the sixth grade, and she was always glad to see a guy who was growing. "You could grow to be as tall as a runway model," her mother always told her, "and those girls are as graceful as swans." But Nicki felt more like a flagpole with big feet. She imagined most runway models felt the same way, at least when they were in middle school.

Michelle Vander Hagen came in, conscious as always that she wore the unofficial label of Most Beautiful Girl in the school. She smiled at Mrs. Balian, flashed a dimple at Scott Spence, and waited until the quiet beauty of her presence hushed the noise around her before she chose a seat.

"There she is," Christine said, sighing. "Our sure bet for seventh-grade Fall Festival queen. It's too bad sixth graders can't elect a representative. She'd have a crown in her closet already."

"I don't know if I could stomach having a Queen Michelle for three years," Nicki grumbled. "It's going to be bad enough having her win this year and next."

"She'll probably be on the homecoming court every year in high school, too," Meredith said. "So you'd better get used to being in class with royalty."

"Michelle can be royal all right—a royal pain," Christine said. "She won't play hard in gym, she won't walk outside in the rain, and remember last year when we all went door-to-door selling candy bars? Michelle wouldn't help. She thought she might mess up her hair."

Nicki laughed. "You're just mad because she was on your relay team and you guys came in last place."

Christine folded her arms and pouted. "Thirty-two times! The girl tried to put a basketball into the hoop thirty-two times and *still* didn't get it in! What's the use in being pretty if you're totally useless?"

Corrin Burns bounced into the room next, obviously as stuck on herself as she was last year. She practically pranced to the front of the room, smiling and sashaying to show off her new outfit. If Corrin wore a label at all, it was Miss Flirt of Pine Grove Middle School.

"She might as well say, 'Look at me! Look at me!'" Meredith said. "Doesn't she know people shouldn't flaunt themselves like that?"

"Corrin doesn't know much about people," Christine answered. "She only knows about boys."

Julie Anderson and Heather Linton now surrounded Corrin, cooing and gushing over her hair, her nails, and her clothes like the loyal sidekicks they were. Meredith turned her head away. "I think I'm going to be sick."

Nicki remembered that Meredith had an unpleasant experience with Corrin last year. Just because Meredith is black, Corrin seemed to think Meredith deserved whatever Corrin chose to dish out. Last year Corrin made the mistake of calling Meredith the "n-word" in gym, and sweet, brainy Meredith came within two inches of punching Corrin out.

The late bell finally rang and Mrs. Balian stood up with her attendance roster. She gave friendly smiles to each of the returning students, but her eyes shone with curiosity when she called, "Cushman, Laura." Everyone was curious and peered at Laura, and Nicki felt uncomfortable for her new friend.

But Laura was as comfortable in the sea of seventh-grade faces as she had been when she ordered in French at the restaurant she and Nicki went to after shopping one day. She faced everyone with a smile, shifted her perfect posture slightly, and said, "Here, ma'am."

Mrs. Balian smiled. "It's nice to meet you, Laura. Where did you live before you moved to Pine Grove?"

"Atlanta, Georgia, ma'am. My mother and I moved here this summer after my father died."

"I'm very sorry." Mrs. Balian hadn't counted on hearing bad news. "But we're very glad to have you in school with us."

As Mrs. Balian continued to call the list of names, Nicki couldn't help but notice that a tiny frown now occupied Michelle Vander Hagen's perfect face. Could she possibly consider Laura a contender for the title of Most Beautiful Girl? Michelle had held that unspoken position since fifth grade, but who knew what would happen this year?

Then Nicki overheard the thin voice of Corrin Burns: "A Rolls-Royce? You've got to be kidding!"

Oh brother. Laura had better look out. Michelle might be disturbed by the competition Laura presented, but Perfectly

Beautiful People rarely acted ugly. Corrin Burns, however, didn't know how to keep her mouth shut.

Neither Michelle nor Corrin could possibly like the idea of a new girl who was pretty, sophisticated, *and* rich. Whatever this upcoming year held, there were bound to be a few fireworks.

# Two

Mr. Padgett, the principal, was halfway through his morning announcements over the intercom when in walked another new student. The girl wore a dark skirt, a white blouse, and black shoes—all unusual for a casual seaside Florida town like Pine Grove. But when she lifted her head to hand Mrs. Balian her registration form, the girls noticed she was Asian.

"Japanese?" Nicki whispered.

Christine shook her head. "Chinese, I think."

"Welcome to Pine Grove Middle and our class," Mrs. Balian said, smiling. "Students, this is Kim Park. This is her first week in America."

"She's from Korea," Meredith whispered. "Park is an old and honorable Korean name."

Laura looked at Nicki. "How does she know these things?"

Nicki grinned. Meredith knew almost everything—sometimes Nicki thought the girl must read encyclopedias for fun. Plus, both her parents were professors, so what she didn't know, she could usually find out.

Mrs. Balian looked up from the note Kim had given her. "Kim and her family are here because her mother is on a waiting list for a kidney transplant," she told the class. "Since Kim speaks very little English, let's do everything we can to help her out, okay?"

The bell rang and everyone filed out to go to first-period

classes. Nicki and her friends had all chosen life science for first period, so they headed toward the biology lab.

In the hall the girls passed Corrin Burns, who had backed Kim Park against the wall. Corrin's sharp voice cut through the muffle of the crowd: "I think it's just great that a Japanese girl is here. You Chinks are good in math, right? You'll do my math homework for me, right?" Corrin rocked back on her heels and smiled at Kim. "If you don't help me out, I can get you into real trouble, because my dad works for the American government. Do you understand?"

Kim had bowed her head when Corrin began, but now she lifted her chin and looked away from Corrin as her tear-filled eyes searched for help. "I . . . no . . . speak . . ."

Meredith wasn't about to stand by and watch. "Corrin, you leave her alone," she snapped, stopping by Corrin's side. "Give the girl a break and do your own lousy math homework. If you can, that is."

Corrin flushed and opened her mouth.

Nicki braced herself for an argument—or worse.

Meredith kept glaring at Corrin. "Don't say anything to me, girl." Her dark eyes flashed. "You'll be better off keeping your opinions to yourself."

Corrin snapped her jaw shut and turned, trotting down the hall with her friends as if nothing had happened. Christine and Laura stopped to comfort Kim.

"It's okay," Laura said. "I'm new here, too, and we're both going to do just fine. Don't worry yourself about any little ol' thing."

Kim looked at the four friends, then shook her head. "I can get you into real trouble because my dad works for the American government!"

Nicki gasped as Corrin's exact words, spoken in Corrin's thin voice, came out of Kim's mouth.

Nicki looked at Meredith. "Did I hear that right?"

"Incredible!" Christine said laughing.

Meredith leaned in for a closer look at the new girl. "How'd you do that?"

Kim smiled at Laura. "It's okay," she said in Laura's honeyed tones. "Don't worry yourself about any little ol' thing."

The four girls stared at each other, then collapsed into giggles while Kim smiled and pointed at her registration card. "First period, life science," she said in the unmistakable accent of the school's guidance counselor.

The girls stopped laughing. "You're really something, Kim," Nicki said, "and we'll go with you to your science class. We're all in that class. But about these voices—"

"It's her gift," Laura said.

"It's amazing," Christine said.

"It's a scientific improbability," Meredith said.

"Whatever," Nicki went on, "I think you'd better concentrate on learning the language and keeping the voices to yourself for a while. Some people just wouldn't understand. They might think you're making fun of them."

Meredith had Kim's ability analyzed by the end of the first week of school. "It's mimicry," she explained as the four girls walked to school. "Some birds, parrots for instance, are able to mimic human voices or sing the songs of other birds."

"But Kim isn't a bird," Nicki pointed out.

Meredith shrugged. "Some people are just good mimics. I have to admit Kim's *really* good. I asked my dad and he said that since some people are born with the innate ability to recall the notes of musical pieces—"

"Like Nicki's perfect pitch?" Christine interrupted.

"Sort of. Nicki, you can hear notes or tones and immediately know what they are, can't you?" Nicki nodded. She had been able to tell a G from a D and everything else in between for as long as she could remember.

"Well, there are people who can hear a musical piece and not only know what the notes are, but can also recall them indefinitely. They could hear a piano piece and actually play it, perfectly, even years later. Perhaps Kim was born with the ability to recall the pitches of people's voices."

Meredith paused to brush a stray curl out of her eyes, then looked dreamily off into the distance. "I'd love to use her as my science project. I'm going to call it 'Dixon's Hypothesis of Total Vocal Recall.'"

"What if she doesn't want to be a science project?" Christine asked. "My little brother Stephen tried an experiment on my little brother Casey, and both of them got into trouble."

Nicki laughed. "What did they do?"

"Stephen put peas in Casey's ears to see if they'd sprout. Mom had to take Casey to the doctor to have them taken out and she made Stephen eat three helpings of peas at dinner for a week." Christine grinned. "We haven't had any experiments at our house in a while."

"I'll help Kim with something while she's helping me," Meredith said. "I'll teach her English while I'm studying my hypothesis. She won't mind."

Laura kicked a pebble off the sidewalk. "What good are all those voices? I think it's kind of spooky."

"Are you kidding?" Christine jumped ahead of the others and turned, walking backward. "You could be the life of any party! You could imitate people for hours!"

"I don't think Kim's the life-of-the-party type," Nicki said. "She seems quiet. She hasn't done anything to make any friends."

"She hasn't done anything to make enemies, either," Meredith pointed out. "She isn't rude or hateful and she doesn't make fun of people even though she could. She's probably trying to learn English."

"Sure, just because she can mimic people doesn't mean she understands the language," Laura added.

"My piano teacher is always fussing at me for using my perfect pitch instead of reading all the notes," Nicki said. "Maybe it's too easy for Kim to use her ability without learning what the words mean. We're going to have to help her learn to talk as herself, not everyone else."

"I'd really like to help," Christine said. "Imagine, the girl is in a strange country with a sick mother, surrounded by people who must seem strange."

"Mean people, too," Meredith said. "I'd love to show her that all Americans aren't like Corrin Burns."

"Why not?" Nicki said. "Everyone willing to help Kim learn to speak English, raise your right hand."

Four right hands went up together. It was decided.

—

Mr. Cardoza, the seventh-grade English teacher, walked to the chalkboard and wrote "Research Paper" in bold letters. In his level voice, he explained: "One-half of your grade this grading period will be a research paper. You are to choose any author, living or dead, and write a paper describing his life, his work, and his writing style. You must also read at least one book by this author and include a report on that book. It's almost like two papers in one, so I suggest you get busy. Your papers are due in three weeks." He paused and looked over the class. "Neatness counts. Any questions?"

There were no questions, only groans. But Meredith raised her hand. "Mr. Cardoza, I'd like to do my paper on William Shakespeare."

"That would be fine, Meredith, but wouldn't you rather report on a less prodigious author?"

Some kids snickered at his choice of words, but Nicki knew Meredith and Mr. Cardoza were on the same wavelength. "I think that to do anyone less prodigious than Shakespeare would be a waste of effort," Meredith said, lifting her chin. "Unless you'd like me to study Chaucer."

Nicki shook her head and grinned at Christine. They knew Meredith's father had written *The Compleat Chaucer*, a thick book that was his chief claim to fame. Meredith knew what she liked, and, thanks to her parents, she liked Chaucer and Shakespeare. She'd rather die than do a report on someone too easy, someone alive.

"You may study Shakespeare only if you do a thorough and complete job," Mr. Cardoza told Meredith. "That means you'll have to read one of Shakespeare's plays, and some college students aren't up to that."

"I can do it," Meredith said, bouncing the eraser end of her pencil against her desk. "If you'll give me two extra days for the report."

Mr. Cardoza thought a moment, then smiled. "For such a project, two extra days is fine with me. Everyone else will hand in their papers on Wednesday; I'll expect yours on Friday." He looked up as the bell rang. "If there are no further questions, class is dismissed."

# Three

Three weeks later, after hours of reading and research, Mr. Cardoza's seventh-grade English class assembled with their papers. Because she had spent the summer reading all 1,054 pages of *Gone with the Wind*, Nicki had done her paper on Margaret Mitchell. Her father's secretary at the insurance office had typed it for her.

Mrs. Cushman had her personal assistant type Laura's report on *Jane Eyre* and Charlotte Brontë. Laura carried the book and an embroidered handkerchief everywhere for three weeks.

"The story is just so beautifully *tragic*," she told the other girls, shaking her blonde hair out of her eyes. "Don't you just love to read a book that makes you cry?" She sighed. "I will not have lived unless I have a romance like Jane Eyre's."

Christine's report was handwritten. "I was lucky to get it done at all," she said, dropping into her seat.

Nicki looked at her friend. "What book did you read?"

Christine pulled a book from her backpack and tossed it in Nicki's direction.

"*Cockatiels?*" Nicki asked, laughing. "You read a book on cockatiels?"

Christine sniffed. "Mr. Cardoza didn't say it had to be a *famous* book. I grabbed the first book I could find at home. Mother's breeding cockatiels now, so that's what I grabbed."

"How did you find any information about the author?" Meredith read the book's cover. "Who is Howard S. Smythe?"

"I looked him up on the Internet," Christine said, raising her chin and glaring at Meredith. "I found out everything I needed to know, thank you."

Kim Park entered the room with her head down, as usual, and Nicki wondered how the girl kept from running into things. She sat down in the first seat two rows over. "Hey, Kim," Meredith called. "Did you get your paper done?"

Kim looked up and shyly nodded. "I read *Bridge to Terabithia* by Katherine Paterson."

Christine leaned forward. "Was it a good book?"

"Yes." Kim looked away and nodded. "It was a good book about a boy and his new friend."

*His new friend.* The words echoed in an awkward pause and Nicki felt a stab of guilt. They had been so busy the past three weeks, they hadn't given much thought to their plan of helping Kim with her English. But she was bright and had improved a lot. Maybe she wouldn't really need their help after all.

The bell rang and the shuffling of feet gradually stopped. While Mr. Cardoza silently checked seats against his attendance chart, practically every girl in the room made her own unconscious check—Scott Spence was present and looking good. It was a nice feeling to know the best-looking guy in school sat only a few rows away.

Nicki noticed that Kim was absently doodling on her notebook cover. Instead of the stupid messages or circles most people drew, Kim doodled in little pictures that Nicki figured were part of the Korean language. It was beautiful, artsy doodling, and Nicki wondered what the letters meant.

Suddenly, Corrin Burns burst into the room. "Mr. Cardoza, someone has stolen my research paper! They stole it from my locker and left this in its place!"

She held up a yellow sheet of paper. But it wasn't the color of the paper that was unusual—it was a mark in the lower right-hand corner: a lovely, delicate pair of Oriental figures.

Mr. Cardoza lifted a brow. "Miss Burns, you are late, you are loud, and you've interrupted."

Corrin lifted her chin. "I was going to be on time, but I stopped by my locker to pick up my paper. I worked *so hard* on it, Mr. Cardoza. But I couldn't find it, so I took all my books out and then, at the bottom of my locker, I found *this!*"

She rattled the paper. "But how could someone get into your locker?" Mr. Cardoza asked patiently. "Don't you keep it locked?"

"I left my locker open for about ten minutes this morning so Heather could pick up a book I borrowed," Corrin explained. "Someone must have taken my report then. I didn't notice anything until now. My report is gone and this was on top of my books!"

Nicki made a mental note—didn't Corrin just say that the paper was at the bottom of her locker? How could it be on the bottom and on top of her books at the same time? The girl had better get her story straight.

Mr. Cardoza took the yellow paper. He studied the two tiny black-inked figures curiously, then looked up at the class. "Does anyone know anything about this? Heather, did you see this paper in Corrin's locker this morning?"

Heather looked at Corrin and swallowed hard. "Um, no, I've never seen anything like that in my life. I—"

"The only place I've seen anything like it is on Kim Park's papers," snapped Corrin.

No one else moved or answered. Mr. Cardoza turned back to Corrin. "I'm sorry, Miss Burns, and I don't know what to do about this. Did you happen to keep a copy—perhaps on your home computer?"

Corrin shook her head. "I didn't think anyone would steal it."

"Well, if I were you, I'd concentrate on rewriting your paper and not making foolish accusations. If I give you another day, can you rewrite your paper from your notes?"

"No," Corrin wailed. "I'll need at least two days."

Mr. Cardoza sighed. "If I give you two days, I will expect the best paper you've ever produced. Agreed?"

Corrin made a point of glaring at Kim, then she nodded to Mr. Cardoza. She slipped into her desk, and Julie Anderson and Heather Linton leaned over to whisper encouragement.

"Miss Dixon." Mr. Cardoza looked at Meredith. "Am I still to receive your Shakespeare paper on Friday?"

"Yes, Mr. Cardoza. I've just finished reading *Hamlet*."

"Excellent." The teacher looked around at the rest of the class and cleared his throat. "Would everyone else please pass your papers forward?"

Meredith leaned toward Nicki. "Why would someone leave a yellow paper with a mark on it in Corrin's locker?" she whispered. "If they really wanted her paper, which is crazy, why wouldn't they just take it?"

"Maybe someone just doesn't like Corrin," Christine said. "That's easy to understand."

"I'm not wild about the girl," Laura said, "but I'd never take her paper."

Christine grinned. "Okay—maybe someone took it because they *hate* Corrin."

"Maybe someone is having trouble in English and needed a paper so they could get ideas," Meredith said. "And maybe someone has this idea, perhaps from another culture, that it's okay to take something if you leave something in its place."

Nicki couldn't believe what Meredith was hinting. "Are you saying Kim took Corrin's paper?"

"What about the little Oriental symbols? You know Kim writes in Korean all the time."

"Yeah, but she's not so stupid as to take something and leave a calling card!" Nicki shook her head. "Besides, I don't think she'd steal anything. I don't think it's right to steal in *anyone's* culture."

"You don't know that it's not perfectly ordinary in Korea to borrow," Meredith argued. "Maybe she thought taking Corrin's paper was sort of a compliment. Maybe she was planning to return it."

"Maybe that's what the funny writing means," Laura said. "IOU or something."

"If she wanted to take a good English paper, she'd take yours." Nicki nodded to Meredith. "You're the only one who gets *As* from Mr. Cardoza."

Christine cleared her throat. "Hello? Anyone listening? Have any of you considered that maybe Kim took it because she doesn't like Corrin?"

Nicki looked over at Corrin, who was making faces at Kim's back. "Well, it's obvious that Corrin doesn't like Kim."

"Are we going to help that girl or not?" Christine said. "We said we were going to help Kim out."

"We were going to help her with her English," Meredith said. "That was our promise. We didn't say anything about defending her from Corrin Burns."

"Well, maybe she needs defending." Nicki crossed her arms. "If Kim took the paper, we need to teach her that taking someone's paper is wrong. If she didn't take it, she'll need our help because it looks like Corrin is going to make her life miserable."

"She could do it," Meredith muttered. "The girl is a witch."

Nicki looked up. Mr. Cardoza had finished stacking their research papers, and in a minute he'd call for quiet.

"Okay, then," she said. "Our fearless foursome will take on a new project after class. Meredith, why don't you and Laura ask Mr. Cardoza for a closer look at that yellow paper? Chris, you come with me and let's talk to Kim. Maybe we can solve this little mystery right away."

—

Christine and Nicki caught up with Kim after class. Nicki tapped on the girl's shoulder to get her attention. "Kim, we'd like to find out what happened to Corrin's research paper. Do you know anything about it?"

Talking to Kim wasn't easy. First of all, she was so shy she kept ducking her head, and Nicki always found it hard to talk to people who wouldn't look her in the eye. "Look directly at people," her parents always told her. "You'll look like you have confidence." Since both her parents were confident salespeople, Nicki figured eyeballing people was high on their priority list.

But Kim wouldn't stop walking down the hall. She wouldn't look up, either, which didn't say much for her confidence.

When she didn't answer Nicki, Christine plunged in: "Kim, we hope you're getting along okay here in school and we want to make things easier for you. Where are you going, your locker?"

Kim kept her head down, but she nodded. Christine smiled. "Okay, let's go to your locker."

Nicki didn't know how to begin. "Do—do you like America?" she stammered. "Is school here a lot like school in Korea?"

Kim had begun to unlock her lock, but she stopped twirling

the combination long enough to look up and smile. "We go to school six days a week in Korea. Only five days here. Students must wear uniforms in Korea. And girls go to one school, boys to another. This"—she looked up and nodded at the confusion around them—"is strange."

Christine and Nicki grinned at each other. Good! That was the most Kim had said since they had met her. As Kim continued to dial her combination, Nicki saw Meredith and Laura rushing toward them, the yellow paper in Meredith's hand. Mr. Cardoza must have given it to them.

"I'm so glad you like school." Nicki smiled at Kim, who snapped the lock and opened the door. "We wanted to—"

She stopped in midsentence as Kim's locker opened. A pile of folded yellow papers fell out onto the floor.

Laura, Meredith, Christine, and Nicki stood with their mouths open. Kim seemed bewildered, and she dug under the papers still in her locker for her science book.

Meredith knelt by the papers on the floor and held the paper next to the others. "It's the same kind of paper," she said. "The same shade of yellow, the same thickness, the same everything."

"Kim," Nicki asked gently, "are these your papers?"

Kim looked at the pages on the floor. "My papers? My locker," she said shrugging, "my papers." Then, in Meredith's voice she said, "The same shade of yellow, the same thickness, the same everything."

Nicki felt horrible. The yellow papers were Kim's. She must

have taken Corrin's research paper. She had practically admitted it.

"Sixty seconds till the bell," Meredith announced. Her inner clock was never wrong, so the girls snapped out of their shock. Before they left, Nicki took one of the yellow papers from the floor and asked Meredith for the paper from Corrin's empty folder. She didn't know what to do next.

# Four

A cloud of gloom hung over the girls as they walked home. "What should we do?" Nicki asked. "Should we tell Mr. Cordoza that we think Kim took Corrin's essay?"

"Maybe we should tell Corrin," Laura suggested. "It was her paper."

"If Corrin got in trouble, she probably deserved it," Meredith said. "She was giving Kim a hard time the other day, remember? Maybe this was a case of payback."

Christine lifted her hand. "Whenever one of us kids is in trouble at home, my dad always says, 'You're innocent until proven guilty!'" Her father was the principal of Pine Grove Christian School, as well as the father of six, so Nicki guessed he had a lot of experience with proving guilt. "In our house, it's hard to tell who did what, and believe me, my older brother and sister have tried to frame us younger kids lots of times."

Laura sighed. "Well, Kim needs someone to help her, that's for sure. I'd hate to be new in school and not have anyone stick up for me." She smiled at the others. "Y'all have been super and I appreciate everything you've done to make me feel at home."

Meredith and Nicki smiled at Laura while Christine threw an arm around her. "It's a pleasure to have you with us, kiddo," Christine said. "I never knew anyone who rode to school in a limo could be, you know, a real person."

Laura smiled. "Yeah, I'm a real person," she said, "and Kim is, too. I think we ought to help her."

"Even if she took Corrin's paper?" Meredith looked down the sidewalk. "Could we trust a friend like that?"

"Maybe she doesn't understand the way we do things over here," Christine answered. "We can work with her and teach her what's cool and what's not."

"Maybe our foursome needs to be a fivesome," Nicki said, thinking out loud. "Okay, even if she did take Corrin's paper, we'll stand by our promise to help her. Agreed?"

"Agreed," Laura said.

Christine nodded. "Ditto."

Meredith sighed. "Okay, I'll agree."

—

The next morning as the girls walked onto the school grounds, they noticed that the crowd of kids who usually hung around outside were streaming into the building. "Are we late?" Christine asked.

"No way." Meredith didn't even check her watch. "We have at least ten minutes until the warning bell."

Nicki walked faster. "Something's up. Let's check it out."

They followed the flow of students to the open area where the lockers were. At the center of the crowd stood a wailing Corrin Burns.

"I'm cursed, I tell you!" she yelled at Mr. Padgett, the principal. "Yesterday my research paper was stolen and today this *thing* has been painted on my locker. It's a curse! Someone is out to get me!"

Mr. Padgett kept saying that curses were sheer nonsense but someone was guilty of vandalism and he'd find out soon enough who it was, thank you very much. As he muttered about suspensions and detentions, the kids closest to the scene of the crime walked away. Nicki and her friends squeezed into the gap.

Corrin's locker door was now adorned with the same Oriental figures they had seen on the yellow sheet of paper. But this time someone had painted them boldly with black spray paint.

"Move on, everybody," Mr. Padgett boomed above the noise. "Everyone go to your locker and then get on to homeroom."

In Mrs. Balian's homeroom, rumors were flying fast and furiously. "The curse of the dragon lady," Natalie Martin whispered to Jansen Moore. "I think it's some kind of occult thing."

Holly Phillips moaned to Michelle Vander Hagen. "It means three days of terrible, awful bad luck. Corrin says she's afraid to get out of bed tomorrow."

Jeff Jordan stood up and looked at the group. "Where'd the curse come from?" he asked. Twenty heads turned in his direction, then twenty pairs of eyes nodded silently toward Kim Park, who sat in the front row.

"This is ridiculous," Nicki snapped, hearing the comments around her. "How can anyone believe Corrin's story about a curse?"

Meredith shrugged. "You know how rumors are. By the end of the day she'll be cursed with three *years* of bad luck."

Christine giggled. "Or have three *ears* growing out of her head!"

"Nonsense," Nicki mumbled, but she had to smile. Especially when Corrin came into the room and trudged toward her seat, pale and shaken, with Heather and Julie clinging to her arms as if at any moment they expected Corrin to take her last breath.

Corrin nodded weakly at her classmates and fluttered her lashes in Scott Spence's direction, then managed a weak glare at the back of Kim Park's head.

Laura groaned. "I think I'm going to be sick."

"I think I'm going to do something about this," Nicki said. "It's silly for Kim to sit up there in the front where people can do things behind her back."

Nicki walked to the front of the room and crossed to Kim's desk. "Kim, why don't you come sit with us? There's an extra seat in our corner of the room."

Kim blushed, bowed her head, and looked up again. "This seat is *not good*?"

"No." Nicki lifted Kim's books from the desk. "This seat is *not* good. Come with me."

Kim followed and Nicki pointed out an empty desk against the wall and behind Christine. Now if anyone made faces in Kim's direction, at least she'd be able to see what was going on.

The bell rang, the announcements were given, the class stood to say the pledge. Mrs. Balian was busy grading papers at her desk as the students waited for the dismissal bell to ring. Usually everyone huddled and talked quietly in little groups, but today Corrin was the center of attention.

"I don't really know if it's a curse," she admitted in her nasal voice. "I suppose it could be some kind of weird coincidence."

"How can that symbol on your locker be a coincidence?" Julie Anderson asked. "Why was it on your locker?"

Corrin shrugged. "I don't know. I don't know why anybody would have anything against me. But there are some really nasty people in the world, people who aren't like us. I mean, just over there . . ." She leaned toward her friends, then looked at Kim.

But like everyone else, Kim had been watching Corrin's dramatic display. When their eyes met, Kim opened her mouth and in Corrin's oboe voice said, "But there are some really nasty people in the world."

Corrin's eyes opened wide, then she slumped over her chair in a dead faint.

# Five

After Corrin came around, waving and flailing her arms, Mrs. Balian wrote her a pass to go see the school nurse. "Tell her to let you go home," Mrs. Balian said. "Anyone sick enough to faint is sick enough to go home."

Corrin put the back of her hand to her forehead and protested, then glanced over to see if Scott Spence was watching. "Mrs. Balian, I'm okay now. I think I can make it through the day." She paused to heave a huge sigh. "Especially if someone could help me carry my books."

"Hrmphfff." Michelle Vander Hagen's disgust showed on her face.

"No, Corrin, tell the nurse to let you go home." Mrs. Balian waved Corrin toward the door. "We'll see you tomorrow if you're feeling better."

Corrin dragged toward the door. "Tomorrow! Under this curse, I'll probably be hit by a school bus! I won't live through tomorrow!"

Meredith groaned as the door closed. "What an act!"

"Do you think she was acting?" Laura's eyes were wide. "I've never seen anyone faint before . . . except my grandmother. She faints any time there's a crisis. Corrin's faint looked real to me."

"Maybe it was partly real and partly fake," Nicki said. "Maybe she was so surprised to hear Kim answer in her own voice that she pretended to faint to cover her surprise."

"No one else seemed to notice Kim's little part in the drama," Christine pointed out. "Everybody was so busy trying to figure out if Corrin was cursed that no one but us was paying any attention to Kim."

"Maybe Corrin's fainting was part of the curse," Laura added. "You know—maybe the curse made her faint."

Meredith elbowed Laura. "You don't really believe she's cursed, do you? That's impossible."

"We're forgetting someone." Nicki pointed to Kim. Ever since Nicki had invited Kim to sit by them, she remained near the girls, watching and listening. Kim was watching now, her pretty, dark eyes alert.

Nicki smiled at Kim. "Do you know anything about a curse?" Kim shook her head.

Nicki pulled out a sheet of notebook paper and tried her best to imitate the two black Oriental figures they had seen on the yellow paper and on Corrin's locker. "Do you know what this means?"

Kim studied the figures for a moment, then shook her head. "Not Korean," she said. "Perhaps Chinese?"

Meredith lifted a brow. "But what does it mean?"

Kim smiled. "I am not Chinese. I am Korean."

Meredith shook her head. "Sorry."

The bell rang and the girls gathered their books. "What do you think?" Nicki whispered to Meredith. "If she doesn't know what the sign means, she didn't write it."

"But what if she's lying?" Meredith protested. "She could be trying to throw us off the track."

Nicki shook her head. The mystery of the mark was as cloudy as ever, but she couldn't believe Kim would lie to her only friends.

—

Mr. Gilbert, the geography teacher, was full of surprises. "In order to give ourselves a full view of the world," he boomed in his lecture voice, "we're spending this hour in the library. I want you to choose a foreign country and prepare a five-minute oral report on it. These reports will be presented in class, beginning tomorrow."

The entire class groaned. "Come on, it's not so bad," Mr. Gilbert said. "There's just one more thing. Everyone must choose a different country, so let me know which nation you'd like to study. First come, first choice."

Nicki couldn't believe what she was hearing. "Isn't this rather *sudden*?" she asked. "I just spent tons of time in the library for English."

"Maybe Mr. Gilbert has a crush on the new librarian," Christine said. She batted her lashes. "Didn't you notice her name is *Miss* Phillips?"

"More like Mr. Gilbert was too busy last night to prepare his lesson plans," Meredith added. Being the daughter of two professors, she would know about such things. "The library is a *great* place for teachers to kill time."

Nicki snapped her fingers. "I have an idea! Maybe through our reports we can find out something about Corrin's mystery mark. We'll sign up right away and choose the Asian countries. Meredith, you choose China. Laura, why don't you take Taiwan? Christine, you take Japan, and I'll take Korea. Okay?"

"I was sort of hoping to study Paris," Laura said, sighing. "My mom says she'll take me there next summer if I do well in school."

"Paris isn't a country, it's a city in France," Meredith pointed out. "And Nicki's idea is good. Okay, everybody?"

The girls nodded. Everyone, that is, but Kim, who asked, "What do I study?"

"Kim," Nicki said, thinking aloud, "why don't you ask Mr. Gilbert if he'll let you study the United States?"

—

The girls split up in the library and Nicki brought the "K" volume of the encyclopedia to the table where she was working. Under "Korea" she skimmed the subheadings: history, population, geography, and climate. Nothing about curses. Rats.

Maybe she could find some information online.

Scott Spence slid into the empty chair across from her. "Hi." Nicki thought of the looks she'd be getting if Corrin or Michelle Vander Hagen were watching. "Hi yourself. What country did you choose?"

Scott grinned. "Canada."

"Why Canada?"

He shrugged. "I was going to study Newfoundland because I have a Newfoundland dog. A Newfie." He laughed and his face turned a light shade of pink. "But Newfoundland isn't a country. I found out it's a province in Canada."

Nicki couldn't stop a giggle. When the librarian looked her way, she lowered her voice. "What's a Newfie?"

Scott flipped through the pages of his encyclopedia, volume "N," then pushed the book toward her. "See for yourself."

A picture of the biggest, blackest, furriest dog in the world covered the page. "Wow! You have one of these?"

Scott gave her a proud smile. "You bet. Over 150 pounds of pure muscle and champion dog."

"What's his name?"

"Pine Grove's Valiant McArthur."

Nicki had to bite her tongue to keep from laughing. "All that name for one dog?"

"Of course." Mr. Gilbert walked by and Scott stopped talking to rustle some papers. When the teacher had moved on, Scott said, "You don't give a dinky little name to a dog like McArthur."

"Is that what you call him? I mean, you don't go out and say, 'Here, Pine Grove's whatever-whoever-whenever.'"

"We call him Mack."

"Well, that's a dinky little name, isn't it?"

Scott leaned toward her. "Is a Mack truck a dinky little truck?"

Nick shook her head and grinned. The guy had a point.

As Miss Phillips approached, they lowered their eyes and pretended to concentrate on their encyclopedias.

"What country did you choose?" Scott asked when the coast was clear.

"Korea."

"Why?"

Nicki thought better of mentioning the mystery. "Because Kim's from Korea."

"Oh yeah?" Scott thought a moment. "She's really cute. Lots of the guys think so."

"Really?" Any of the girls would give up half their wardrobe to hear Scott say they were cute, but Nicki thought Kim would probably be embarrassed.

"Yeah."

—

"Scott Spence told me he thought Kim was really cute," Nicki told Meredith, Laura, and Christine after school as they stood by the lockers. "Should I tell her?"

"Oh yes!" Laura said. "That'd make my day."

Christine looked doubtful. "Would it embarrass her?"

"Don't say anything," Meredith said. "You'll only make her feel self-conscious."

"Well, she is cute," Nicki answered. "And more people would see it if she'd lift her head and be more self-confident. Maybe we could help her feel good about herself. We don't have to say it's Scott who thinks she's cute."

"*Who?*" Julie Anderson, who had apparently overheard Nicki's comment, popped around the row of lockers like a jack-in-the-box. "Who does Scott Spence like?"

Christine grinned. "Kim Park."

"Wait, I don't know that he *likes* her," Nicki said, "but I guess he does, as a friend."

Laura smiled at Julie. "He thinks she's beautiful. Isn't that wonderful?"

Julie took off and joined up with Heather Linton and Michelle Vander Hagen on the other side of the lockers. "Now you've done it, Laura," Meredith said. "The news will be every-where in ten minutes."

Laura hugged her notebook to her chest. "I know. It could make things real interesting around here."

—

Nicki didn't know if interesting was quite the word to describe the next day. Corrin Burns was back in school, but she was dressed in black from head to toe. Black hat, black skirt and blouse, black tights, and black combat boots.

As they waited for the tardy bell in homeroom, Jeff Jordan called out, "Hey, Corrin, what's with the outfit? Have you gone Goth or are you in mourning?"

"Don't be an ignoramus," she called over her shoulder. She turned back to her friends. "Some people are so lucky. They will never know how terrifying it is to live under a curse. I only hope it ends today. That dragon chick is the last person on earth I want to deal with!"

Heather Linton punched Corrin as Kim Park walked in, then Heather put her fingers beside her eyes and stretched the skin outward. "Chink warning!"

"Hide me, hide me," Corrin squealed. "How could *anyone* say that witch is cute? I'll never understand it." Corrin ducked under her hat and turned away. Julie Anderson tried to shield Corrin with her notebook while Heather held an oversized geography book over Corrin's face.

"Hi, Kim," Nicki called in a bright voice. "Come on over and sit down." Nicki noticed that Kim's lower lip quivered slightly as she made her way to her seat.

"If the dragon chick comes near you," Corrin said loudly, "you have to raise two fingers in a V and wiggle them, like this."

Corrin lifted two fingers before her own wide eyes, then she whirled to face Kim. Fingers wriggling, she shrieked, "Curses to curses, dragon chick. Curses back to you!"

Did Corrin have any idea how stupid she looked? Nicki was about to say something, but then she saw that Kim's eyes had filled with tears. The poor girl threw her hands over her face and turned toward the wall.

Nicki turned on Corrin and her friends. "That's enough! There's no such thing as a curse, and Kim didn't put one on you."

"Oh sure, Nicki Holland." The brim of Corrin's hat bobbed up and down. "We'll just see about that. Don't mess with things you don't understand. You just might get hurt!"

# Six

In English on Friday, Mr. Cardoza handed back the research papers. Nicki's paper on Margaret Mitchell had earned a B+ and Laura got a B on Charlotte Brontë. "Please clean up the tear stains on your pages, Miss Cushman," Mr. Cardoza had written with his famous purple pen.

Christine got a C on her cockatiel paper. "Ugh, it's bleeding," she moaned. "Just look at all that purple ink." Across the top of her paper, Mr. Cardoza had scrawled, "Really now, is this great literature?"

The remark offended Christine. "To my mother and her birds, this is great stuff."

"I believe I need two additional papers," Mr. Cardoza reminded the class. "Miss Burns and Miss Dixon, are your papers ready?"

Corrin handed Mr. Cardoza a black folder. "It's all there," she said, lifting her chin. "The best thing I've ever done, just like you said."

Meredith was still digging through her book bag.

"Miss Dixon?"

She looked up, her eyes wide. "I can't find my p-paper!" she stammered. "I know I had it here in my book bag. It has to be here somewhere!"

"I am growing tired of this disappearing paper theme," Mr. Cardoza remarked, his voice dry. "Miss Dixon, you have until the end of the day to bring me your paper. Perhaps you will find it in your locker."

Meredith sat numbly, not moving. Finally, she nodded.

"Meredith, where could you have left your paper?" Nicki whispered. "Do you want us to help you look for it?"

"There's no sense in looking. It's gone." Meredith's eyes were dark and distant. "Look what I found in my book bag." Meredith pulled out a folded sheet of yellow paper. She unfolded it, but Nicki already knew what they would see inside: the mysterious mark of the curse.

—

For a girl who had been cursed, Nicki realized, Corrin Burns was enjoying better luck than anyone else on Friday.

By the time the group met together in geography, Meredith was a wreck. Corrin, who wouldn't have to give an oral report because she'd had the good fortune to faint the day it was assigned, sat at her desk, cool as a cucumber.

Even more unlucky for Meredith, hers was the first name Mr. Gilbert called. Was it because he knew she'd be ready? If so, maybe being supersmart was a curse in itself.

Meredith got up and gave a good five-minute summary of China, which wasn't easy because, as she pointed out, China has more people and probably more history than any other nation on earth.

As she passed Nicki on her way back to her seat, Meredith whispered: "And no, I didn't learn anything about curses or symbols. If that symbol is Chinese, it is one of thousands of Chinese figures in two or three dialects. And I still haven't found my research paper."

Meredith propped up her geography book and began trying to rewrite her paper on Shakespeare and *Hamlet* from memory while Jansen Moore reported on Australia in a fake and very poor Aussie accent.

Christine crinkled her freckled nose. "He's just trying to sound like the Crocodile Hunter."

Mr. Gilbert called Nicki next. She shuffled her notes and walked to the front of the room, quickly running her tongue over the front of her teeth. Last year she had seen a guy give an oral report with a chunk of Dorito stuck to his front tooth. Nicki *never* wanted that to happen to her.

"I chose to do my report on South Korea because our new friend, Kim, is Korean," Nicki said. "The Koreans are a proud people. It is a country blending change with old traditions. The more common family names are Kim, Lee, Park, Chung, and Han. A woman does not change her name when she is married."

Nicki looked up from her notes. At her desk, Kim was smiling. Good. Nicki wanted to do a good job for her friend's sake.

"Seoul, the capitol of South Korea, is a modern city with subways, highways, taxis, hotels, and the athletic centers of the 1988 Olympics. It has many fine restaurants. The people like to eat rice, mainly, and a dish made from pickled cabbage called kimchi. Food is usually eaten mixed together."

She heard several "yucks" and looked up with a smile. "The food is good," she assured the class. "In open-air markets people can buy ducks, live chickens, or even dogs."

She wasn't quite prepared for the reaction.

"Gross!"

"That's awful!"

"They eat dogs?"

"Totally disgusting!"

Mr. Gilbert rapped a ruler on his desk. "Don't judge every culture by your own," he reminded them. "Remember that snails are a delicacy in France; ants, worms, and beetles are considered fine foods in Africa."

"Ugghhhhh!" everyone groaned.

"Those people aren't like us," Corrin Burns said. "Sometimes I think we're the only people in the world with any sense."

Mr. Gilbert frowned. "Perhaps they think it's a shame we aren't more like them," he said. "Nicki, please continue."

"My five minutes are almost up," Nicki said, grateful that the uproar had killed some time. "There are two important birthdays in the life of a Korean—the first and the sixtieth, when the cycle of active life is completed. Korea, and Koreans, are interesting."

Everyone applauded politely and Nicki went back to her desk.

"Next," Mr. Gilbert called, looking at his class list. "Scott Spence will report on Canada. Scott?"

Scott sighed and reached for his notebook.

"Uh-oh."

"What's wrong, Scott?" Mr. Gilbert asked.

"Don't tell me," Christine muttered. "His report is missing."

Scott held up his report. It wasn't missing, but someone had covered his notes with the now-famous mystery mark. Some kind of heavy black marker had totally covered Scott's work.

Mr. Gilbert looked at Scott over the top of his glasses. "Scott, is this some kind of trick to get out of giving your report?"

Scott shook his head, but no one noticed because just then Corrin jumped out of her seat, two fingers raised and wriggling in that crazy sign she'd invented. "It's the curse," she shouted. "It's been passed on to you, Scott! Look out! For the next three days I'd stay home! She did it to you—the dragon chick!"

—

After Meredith took her quickly written Shakespeare report to Mr. Cardoza, she met Christine, Laura, Nicki, and Kim by their lockers. "Listen, let's get together tonight," Nicki suggested. "Whose mother will let us come over?"

Christine rolled her eyes. "My mother wouldn't care, but with all the noise at my house we wouldn't get anything done."

Meredith shook her head. "Tonight is supposed to be my night at my dad's apartment and he's not up to having a bunch of girls over. But he wouldn't care if I went somewhere."

"My mom and dad probably wouldn't mind," Nicki said, "but Mom's showing a house tonight and Dad's trying to sell insurance to some new neighbors."

Laura smiled. "Well, then, it's settled. My mom and I would love to have y'all over. Kim, are you sure you can come?"

Kim smiled, a pretty flush shining through her pale skin. "I will ask," she said. "This is a slumber party? We will sleep?"

Meredith grinned. "Sort of. We'll talk a lot and sleep a little. It'll be fun."

"Mother will send the car to pick you all up," Laura said. "Be ready at six, okay?"

Kim waved good-bye as she went to meet her bus, and the other girls gathered their books to walk home.

Suddenly an angry voice destroyed the after-school silence: "I'm getting a little tired of this!"

Nicki and the others sprinted past three rows of lockers until they saw Scott Spence scowling. "It was bad enough that my report was ruined, but now I'll probably have to pay to have my locker repainted!"

Someone had spray-painted Scott's locker with the mystery mark, and recently, too, because a messy drip was now running onto the locker beneath his.

Nicki looked around. No one in sight.

She turned to Scott. "Did you see anyone come by here?"

"School's been out for ten minutes," Scott reminded her. "*Everybody's* been by here."

"Does anyone see any other clues?" Meredith asked.

Aside from the usual trash left at the end of the day, Nicki saw nothing unusual.

Laura cleared her throat. "Well, Kim was with us," she said, "so we know *she* didn't do it."

"Actually, she had just left us," Meredith pointed out. "She has been gone about four minutes, and this paint *is* fresh."

Nicki frowned. "Scott, this mark was also on your report, right? Well, did you leave your notebook lying around at any time today or yesterday? How could someone have marked your report?"

Scott ran his fingers through his hair. "That's crazy, Nicki. All of us leave our notebooks out sometimes. We stash them on that empty table at lunch, and just this morning I left my notebook on the sidewalk while we were riding Jeff Jordan's skateboard."

"Why don't you just keep your notebook with you?" Christine asked.

Scott shrugged. "You ever try boardin' with a notebook in your hand? Besides, you don't expect anyone to sabotage your homework." He laughed. "And anyone who stole mine would be crazy—my stuff's not that good."

Nicki smiled at his joke. "Well, it's a shame about your locker. Mr. Padgett is going to be upset that it happened again."

"Whoever did it is gone now," Scott said, carefully opening his locker without touching the wet paint. "Wait—here's something else!"

On top of Scott's books and rolled-up gym towel lay a folded sheet of yellow paper—identical, it seemed, to those the girls had already seen in Kim's locker. It was also identical to the papers left for Meredith and Corrin.

Scott carefully unfolded the paper. The mystery mark occupied the center of the page, but on this paper there were also two words written in block letters: DOG MEAT.

# Seven

"Dog meat?" Scott looked at Nicki. "What in the world does that mean?"

"It could mean that *you're* dog meat," Christine answered. "My brother Tommy says that every time he threatens my little brothers. Does someone want to beat you up?"

"It could have something to do with *eating* dog meat," Meredith said, her eyes thoughtful. "Sort of like saying to someone, 'Go eat nails.' Maybe in another culture they say, 'Go eat a Chihuahua.'"

Meredith leaned to whisper in Laura's ear: "Maybe a certain young lady got embarrassed because she heard Scott thinks she's cute."

Laura gasped. "You can't believe that! Would you get mad if Scott said you were cute?"

"Maybe—if I were shy and the whole school was talking about me."

Nicki took the paper from Scott. "Maybe the letters mean something else. They could be jumbled together or in code." She looked at him. "Do you mind if we take this? We're all staying at Laura's tonight. We're sort of investigating the strange happenings around school."

Scott grinned. "Gonna be investigators, huh?"

Nicki noticed that the other girls were looking at her with

curiosity—they were probably wondering when she and Scott had become so friendly.

Let them wonder. She looked at him again. "Yeah, something like that. We're trying to help Kim get adjusted to life in Pine Grove."

Scott frowned. "You don't believe Corrin's story about a curse, do you?"

Meredith snapped her gum. "Corrin's already got too many other people believing her nutty ideas. Of course there's no such thing as a curse. Someone's just making trouble, that's all."

Scott closed his locker. "Well, good luck, Nicki Holland and company. Let me know if I can do anything to help."

As Scott walked away, Laura called out a warning. "Be careful! You found the mystery mark! There are still two and a half days of the curse left!"

Meredith gaped at her friend. "You don't really believe in the curse, do you? I mean, I found one of those marks in my book bag and no matter what happens, I refuse to believe three days of bad luck are waiting for me."

Laura shook her head and set her blonde curls dancing. "I don't believe in a curse—at least, I don't think I do. 'Specially not one from Kim Park. But someone has their heart set on making trouble for Corrin, Scott, and you. Doesn't that worry you even a little bit? I'd be scared spitless."

"Nothing's gonna happen," Meredith snapped. "It's the weekend. So far everything bad has happened here at school, and we'll be home this weekend." She lowered her voice so only Nicki could hear. "Plus, we'll have Kim with us. Nothing else can happen."

—

After the girls had been picked up by Laura's chauffeur and fed hand-tossed pizza by the Cushmans' cook, they relaxed in Laura's room. Or perhaps suite would be a better description, Nicki realized. The bedroom had an adjoining sitting room with two couches, a table, television, computer desk, DVD player, and treadmill. A connecting bathroom was bigger than Nicki's bedroom—*and* it had a fireplace!

Meredith stood in the center of the space, her arms out and her eyes as round as dinner plates. "This place is fantastic! This is bigger than my bedrooms at my mom's and my dad's put together!"

"I'd shave my head for a room like this," Christine said, twirling in the spaciousness. "I can't believe it! I've shared a room with at least one sister for as long as I can remember. And all of this is just for you?"

Laura blushed. "There's really just me and Mother in the house. My sister April goes to boarding school in Vermont, so when she's home she stays in the guest room downstairs."

Nicki smoothed a tiny wrinkle out of the peach-flowered chintz bedspread. "Where's Kim? Did we lose her?"

Kim stepped out of Laura's cavern of a closet. "I'm sorry," she said, blushing. "I've never seen a room just for clothes and shoes."

"It's a closet, Kim," Meredith said. "That's a closet, but it's probably the biggest one in Pine Grove."

Laura giggled. "My mother's is bigger."

The girls laughed, but stopped when the soft voice and gardenia fragrance of Virginia Louise Cushman floated into the room. "I'm so glad you all have come," she said, her soft complexion blending perfectly with Laura's peach-colored furnishings. "Nicki, it's really a delight to see you again. Laura, can I have the pleasure of meeting your other friends?"

Laura introduced Meredith, Christine, and Kim, and Mrs. Cushman shook each of their hands. "Well, girls, I'm going to retire early tonight," she said. "If there's anything at all you need, please let me or Mrs. Perkins know."

Nicki remembered her manners. "Thank you, Mrs. Cushman, for having us over. You have a lovely home."

Everyone murmured their agreement and Mrs. Cushman smiled. "Thank you, girls. You are such lovely friends for Laura."

A faint scent of gardenia lingered after she left, but the spell was broken when Laura grabbed a pillow from her bed and ran toward her sitting room. "Last one to the meeting has to take notes," she called.

Two hours later, no one had taken any notes, but each girl had filled a notebook page with doodles. Nicki found it difficult to discuss the mystery in front of Kim, whom Meredith kept referring to as "Suspect Number One." Nicki didn't really believe Kim was guilty of stealing, lying, and vandalism, but somehow the mystery did seem to revolve around her.

"Maybe we should set some goals," Nicki said. "'We're getting nowhere."

"Right," Meredith agreed. "And since I'm nearing the first deadline on my science project, I think we should test the scope of Kim's vocal mimicry."

Laura made a face at Meredith, then smiled at Kim. "Would that be okay with you?"

Kim looked a little uncertain, but she nodded. "I want to help my new friends."

"Get comfortable," Meredith told her, so Kim leaned back on the couch and tucked her legs under her.

"Okay, begin the experiment."

At Meredith's instruction, the girls said various words and phrases to hear how Kim would answer. Christine tried her Irish accent, modeled on her Aunt Milly. Kim answered, sounding not like Aunt Milly, but exactly like Christine imitating Aunt Milly.

Laura smiled. "Can you do my mother?"

When Kim opened her mouth, they all heard Mrs. Cushman saying, "Thank you, girls. You are such lovely friends for Laura." Her words sounded so much like Mrs. Cushman, Nicki could almost smell gardenia perfume.

Laura shivered. "That's spooky."

Meredith's father had taught her how to speak an old English dialect, so she began reciting Chaucer: "Whan that Aprill with his shoures soote, the droghte of March hath perced to the roote . . ."

Kim recited the poem back, word for word, tone for tone, exactly as Meredith had said it.

"Amazing," Nicki said. "I can turn my back on you two and not know which one of you is talking."

"I have one final test," Meredith said. She turned on the television and pressed the controls until she found a news broadcast.

Tom Brokaw filled the screen. "This is Tom Brokaw with a special report," he said.

Meredith looked at Kim. "Can you do him?"

Kim closed her eyes and said in her own voice: "This is Tom Brokaw with a special report." Her presentation was similar, but her voice simply didn't have the depth she needed to imitate a man.

"That's the catch," Meredith said, pulling a pencil from behind her ear. "Kim's voice isn't low enough to imitate a man's. She can do women and children perfectly, but not men."

Nicki smiled at Kim. "Hey, Kim, can we play a little guessing game?"

Kim raised a brow. "What kind of game is this?"

"You say something, anything, that you've heard people say around school. We'll try to guess who said it. Okay?"

Kim nodded and closed her eyes. "Okay, I thought of one."

She took a deep breath. "Jeff Jordan, isn't this your third tardy this week?"

Christine clapped. "I got it, that's Mrs. Balian!" She grinned. "That's unreal."

Kim nodded and closed her eyes again. "If I don't see some action around here immediately, there will be a new list of detentions for next week!"

Even though she was imitating a man, there was no mistaking the principal's clipped accent. The girls laughed. "Mr. Padgett!"

Kim smiled. "I must think of someone harder." She closed her eyes, then smiled. "Rats! Paint on my fingers!"

Nicki looked at Meredith. Meredith looked at Christine. Christine shook her head and looked toward Laura, whose eyes widened.

"Kim, we don't know who that is," Laura said. "Who had paint on their fingers?"

Kim shook her head. "I don't know. I was in the water closet and heard the voice. I couldn't see who spoke."

Christine looked at Nicki. "Water closet?"

"Rest room," Meredith said, translating.

"Did they whisper, just like you did?" Nicki asked.

"Just the same."

"Was anyone else in the bathroom when you came out of the, um, closet?"

"No, no one."

"Did you see anything?" Nicki pressed.

Kim looked a little frightened. "Nothing."

Christine gave her a reassuring smile. "It's okay, no big deal. But do you remember when this happened?"

Kim thought, then nodded. "I remember. Yesterday, after school. We said good-bye, I went to water closet, I mean rest room, and then to my bus. Yesterday."

Meredith looked at Nicki and Nicki could almost see Meredith's mind beginning to work. Had Kim overheard the mysterious troublemaker or was she trying to throw them off the track of what had become a puzzling mystery?

"Time to take a break," Christine called, standing. Nicki knew she was getting restless. "Let's watch the movie I rented."

"Okay," Nicki said, "but after the movie we've got to set another goal. We promised Scott we'd work on this 'dog meat' clue."

The girls were glad to take a break, so for the next two hours they howled through a silly movie about a crime-solving detective and his Chinese pug. Kim cracked them up when she unexpectedly and perfectly imitated the yowling of the dog.

Laura called down to the kitchen from the intercom in her room and soon the housekeeper brought up a gigantic bowl of hot, buttered popcorn. "This is the life," Christine said. "Do you think your mom might want to adopt me? My parents would never miss me."

When the movie was over and all that remained of the popcorn was a few unpopped kernels, the girls settled down to unravel the second part of the mystery.

"DOG MEAT—what does it mean?" Meredith asked. She looked at Kim. "Does anyone have any idea?"

Kim threw her a bewildered look.

Nicki snapped her fingers as a sudden idea hit her. "Hey, Laura, do you have a Scrabble game?"

"Sure. Let me get it."

When Laura brought her Scrabble game from the closet, Nicki turned the game board upside down and then took the letters D O G M E A T out and placed them on the board. "What could you spell with this?"

The girls began pushing and pulling the letters into different combinations. "DOG MEAT could also mean GOD TEAM or DOG MATE," Christine said. "That's silly."

"How about this?" Laura pulled the letters into a different combination: AT DOME G. "Is there a dome anywhere around here?"

"Not that I know of," Nicki said. "I don't think that's it."

"How about GET A MOD?" Christian said. "Or GET A DOM?"

"Could it have something to do with a jewelry robbery?" Meredith asked. "I can spell TOAD GEM. Is there a famous diamond around here called the Toad Gem?"

Laura giggled. "I don't think there are any famous toady gems around our school."

Nicki moved the Scrabble letters around again. "This could be scary. How about MET G DOA?"

Laura crinkled her nose. "What does that mean?"

"Someone with the initial G was met at the hospital dead on

arrival—DOA. I've seen little notes like that on my dad's desk when he's settling someone's life insurance policy."

"I don't think this is a message in code," Meredith said. She sat up and stretched. "And I'm so tired my brain is turning to mush. Anyone for a late-night creature feature?"

Somewhere during *Godzilla's Attack on the Amazon Women*, everyone but Nicki dozed off. She couldn't help feeling they were staring at something important and had missed it.

Sometimes the thing you were looking for was right in front of your nose.

# Eight

At ten o'clock the next morning, Mrs. Perkins, the house-keeper, gently shook Nicki's shoulder. "Hon, there's a telephone call for you. You can take it on the phone in Laura's room, if you like."

Nicki had fallen asleep on one of the sofas in Laura's sitting room, and she had to step over Kim and Meredith, who were sleeping on the floor. She lifted the handset and struggled to keep her eyes open. "Hello?"

"Nicki? This is Scott Spence. Sorry to bother you at Laura's."

Nicki became wide awake. What in the world did Scott want at ten o'clock on a Saturday morning? She could feel herself blushing, and she was glad the other girls were asleep.

"The curse has struck again," Scott said. "Mack is gone. Vanished into thin air." Scott's voice held a worried note. "Dog meat, remember? Do you think that had something to do with Mack?"

"Wait a minute, slow down. Who's Mack?" Her brain felt cloudy, still fogged by sleep, Godzilla, and late-night giggles.

"McArthur, my dog. Remember?"

"Oh yeah, now I remember. What do you mean, he vanished? Did you see him disappear?"

"I put him out this morning like I always do, but when I called him to come in, he wasn't in the backyard. He was gone. It's the second day of the curse and my dog is gone."

"Wait a minute, Scott. Did you check the fence? Could he have dug under the fence?"

"I checked. No holes, and the gate was closed."

"Well . . . could someone have stolen him?"

"Most people are too afraid of him to come near the fence—he's big, you know. I've never had anyone even come up to the gate before."

"But could someone have stolen him? Was the gate locked?"

Scott hesitated. "The gate wasn't locked. And I guess someone *could* have taken him, because even though he looks like a big bear, he's really as friendly as a puppy. Mack likes everybody."

Nicki looked over at Kim, who was still sleeping. At least they knew Kim didn't take Scott's dog.

"Do you think it's the curse, Nicki? Did you guys figure out anything last night?"

"Come on, Scott," Nicki whispered as the other girls began to stir. "You don't really think a curse lifted your dog out of your yard, do you?"

"No, but maybe the curse boils down to three days of bad luck, and my terrible luck happens to be that my dog got stolen. Do you think that's what dog meat means?" Scott was talking faster, growing more upset by the minute. "Do you think Kim Park took my dog? You said they eat dogs in Korea. That note said DOG MEAT."

"Scott, that's crazy. Besides, Kim is here with me. She didn't go anywhere this morning and she isn't eating your dog now. She's asleep."

Scott exhaled over the phone. "I'm calling the police, then."

"Okay, if it'll make you feel better, go ahead. But maybe Mack ran away. Maybe there are too many coincidences and you're feeling spooked. Mack will probably be home in time for supper."

Scott was calmer now, and he hung up after agreeing to call again if anything else happened. Nicki looked around the room where her friends were waking. Kim was just sitting up, calmly watching Laura brush her hair.

Were they wrong about the latest puzzle? Could DOG MEAT really mean dog hamburger? Nicki suddenly felt very sorry she had ever mentioned food in her report on Korea.

# Nine

Christine sat up and looked at Nicki. "Was that who I think it was?"

"It was Scott." Nicki dropped into an overstuffed chair. "His dog is missing and he thinks the curse has something to do with it."

Meredith looked at Kim, then turned back to Nicki. "Well, at least we know Suspect Number One had nothing to do with it. His dog is probably out for a walk."

Nicki glared at Meredith for making the crack about Suspect Number One right in front of Kim, then she settled back to think. "Scott thinks someone might be out there eating his dog."

Christine groaned. "I think I'm going to be sick."

"It's just the popcorn kernels you insisted upon eating," Meredith said. "Now you have tiny pebbles in your stomach."

Nicki sat up as a sudden thought slammed into her brain. "Why don't we go over to Scott's and look around?"

Laura grabbed Nicki's big toe and pulled it playfully. "Is there something you're not telling us? Do you like Scott Spence or something?"

"No more than anyone else." Nicki grinned, reaching for her backpack. "Let's get going. Get dressed and we'll go to Scott's."

Mrs. Cushman was nice enough to provide breakfast and the limo driver for the girls. "I almost feel like we're real private eyes," Christine said as they rode through the streets, munching on doughnuts. "Our own car! Is there anyplace else we need to go? To the mall? To the beach?"

Meredith reached over Christine for another doughnut. "Come back down to earth, Chris. After we go to Scott's, I've got to get home. Dad will be upset if I don't spend any of my weekend with him."

"I need to go home, too," Kim said, her voice soft. "My mother is ill and was kind to let me come last night."

The girls fell silent for a moment, then Laura touched Kim's arm. "How is your mother these days?"

Kim smiled. "She is weak, but waiting. Soon the hospital will call with a kidney, and then my mother will go to the hospital for the operation."

"Is your dad working?" Christine asked.

Kim nodded. "My father is a nuclear engineer and works for a company nearby. We came here to Pine Grove to be near my father's work, but we are a long way from the hospital where my mother will have surgery. Many expenses." Kim shook her head.

The limo pulled up outside Scott's house in Kings' Grant, a large housing development where lots of kids from Pine Grove Middle School lived, including Nicki, Christine, and Meredith—when she was staying with her mom, at least. Scott was sitting on his front lawn, an empty leash in his hand.

"It's no use," he said as the girls walked up. "I've been up and down three different streets and I haven't seen anything of Mack."

Nicki looked at the house. Everything seemed normal. "Can we look around? Laura, why don't you and Kim ask the neighbors if they saw anything. Chris, you check the front, and Meredith and I will check the backyard and the fence."

She caught herself giving orders and blushed. "Sorry," she said, looking down. "I don't mean to be bossy. I'm just used to telling my little brother and sister what to do."

"It's okay," Scott said, standing. "Come on, I'll show you the backyard."

The backyard was surrounded by a chain-link fence, which meant anyone could have seen Mack at any time, Nicki noted. Perhaps someone had been admiring Mack for some time and had simply stolen him.

"Are Newfoundlands expensive?" she asked Scott.

"Usually," Scott answered. "I know what you're thinking —someone might have taken him to sell him. My dad said maybe someone took Mack to use him in illegal dog-fighting. But Mack isn't the fighting type, no matter how big he is."

Meredith had been walking along the edge of the fence. "There aren't any holes under the fence where he could have dug himself out," she reported. "There aren't any holes in the fence, either."

"I didn't see any footprints in the flower beds," Christine said.

Scott grinned. "Did you expect to find some?"

"Policemen always look for footprints in flower beds," Christine said. "But your flower beds are covered in mulch, so they don't show footprints."

"Neither does thick Florida sod." Nicki bit her lip and thought hard. "What time did you let Mack out this morning?"

Scott scratched his head. "He wanted out at seven thirty, then I went back to bed."

"Is that when you usually let him out?"

"On school days I let him out at six thirty when I get up," Scott said. "But everyone in my family sleeps in on Saturday."

"Do you usually let him out on Saturdays at seven thirty?"

"Um, I guess so. Mack likes to get out early. That's pretty much our Saturday routine."

Meredith had more questions. "Does Mack have any enemies? Does he bark and disturb the neighbors? Has he ever bitten anyone?"

Scott shook his head. "Never. Everyone loves Mack. That's why it's so unbelievable that anyone would take him."

Laura and Kim returned from visiting the neighbors. "No one saw anything unusual," Laura said. "No one was up before eight except two little kids across the street. They were watching cartoons."

"I guess we should go now," Nicki told Scott. "We hope Mack comes back, but if this has anything to do with the so-called 'curse,' we'll figure it out soon." She frowned slightly. "I hope."

—

Laura asked the limo driver to take Kim home first. She lived in Levitt Park Apartments and the girls were all a little curious to know more about her.

"Won't you come in?" she asked when the car pulled up by her apartment. Nicki hesitated, but Christine and Laura were quick to accept. "Sure!" Christine practically bounded out of her seat.

Kim knocked on the door and a smiling man opened it. "Ah, Kim." He smiled and opened the door wider. "Please ask your friends to come in."

"I am Park Sang Soo," he said, and Nicki knew he had used the Korean form of placing his last name first. "My wife, Yoo Kyung, is pleased to meet you, too."

A lovely woman in a perfectly white dress sat on the couch and nodded gently toward the girls. "My mother does not speak English," Kim explained. She spoke to her mother in Korean, then smiled at the girls. "Would you like to have some tea?"

"I don't know about this," Meredith whispered to Nicki.

Nicki elbowed her. "Say yes," she whispered back. "It would be rude to say no." She nodded to Kim's mother.

The girls removed their shoes at the door and sat on a straw mat in front of a low table. Kim gave each girl a tea cup, and her father poured a green tea. Christine caught Nicki's eye. This had better be good, her look said, but when Nicki tasted, it was.

When they had finished their tea and their polite conversation with Kim's parents, the girls went into Kim's bedroom. Instead of a normal bed, Kim slept on a pallet made of what looked like satin and silk. The bed was beautifully embroidered and stored rolled up like a sleeping bag.

Kim unrolled the pallet to show the girls. "This is beautiful!" Laura rubbed her hand over the white satin coverlet. "Look at this embroidery!"

Kim smiled. "My mother made it. She makes beautiful things."

"She must be very talented," Meredith said, looking at the quilt.

"Her name, Yoo Kyung, means 'delightful star.'" Kim smiled. "I honor her as my mother."

"I honor my mother, too," Christine said, a thoughtful expression crossing her face. "With six kids, she deserves it."

"With six kids, she needs it," Kim said. Her joke caught the girls by surprise.

Meredith lifted a brow. "Kim, you have a sense of humor!"

"Is that surprising?" Kim asked. "Cannot Suspect Number One be funny?"

# Ten

As the limo pulled away from Kim's apartment, Nicki, Laura, Meredith, and Christine were more than a little embarrassed. They had realized that just because Kim was from another country didn't mean she was stupid. She had known all along that they suspected her of being behind the strange happenings at school. Yet she didn't blame them and seemed to be as interested in solving the mystery as they were.

"Kim didn't do any of it," Nicki told the others. "In order to find the guilty person, you have to first establish that he or she had a motive and an opportunity to commit the crime. Kim has no motive. Plus, she didn't have a chance to take Scott's dog. She was with us."

Meredith leaned forward. "She looked like a good suspect for a while. After all, she had a locker full of yellow papers; she can write an Asian language; and Corrin Burns is so prejudiced Kim has every right to be mad at her. She had a reason to be mad at Scott, too, if she was embarrassed because everyone was saying he thinks she's cute."

"That's crazy," Laura said. "Anyone, including Kim, would be flattered if Scott liked them. Kim didn't have a motive for anything. I don't even think she holds a grudge against Corrin."

Christine looked out the car's tinted window. "Corrin has done nothing but make Kim's life miserable. She yelled at Kim on the first day of school, she calls her 'dragon chick,' and she is still doing that weird stuff with her fingers."

"And her friends give a 'Chink alert' whenever Kim walks by," Laura added. "That's terrible."

"Everyone knows Corrin is prejudiced," Nicki said. "Meredith, remember last year when she called you—"

"I remember," Meredith said. "You don't have to remind me."

Nicki shook her head. "Corrin's always been weird about stuff like that. It's one of the ways she gets attention. I can't believe how many people take her seriously."

Meredith pulled out a sheet of paper. "Okay—if Kim isn't the guilty party, then we can trust her, right? She gave us a couple of clues we ought to track down."

"The voice in the bathroom," Nicki said.

"We couldn't recognize it because she whispered, but it was a girl," Meredith said. "Unless a boy was sneaking into the girls' bathroom."

"Too risky," Christine said. "Nobody I know would do it."

"Then we know our mysterious graffiti artist is a girl," Nicki said. "And we think she is acting alone."

"Practically every girl in our class had the same chance to commit the crime as every other girl," Christine said. "Maybe we should think about motives."

Nicki nodded. "Who would want to hurt Corrin Burns . . . and why?"

Laura wriggled her fingers to catch Nicki's attention.

"Michelle Vander Hagen might be jealous. I've noticed that she doesn't like Corrin's flirting with Scott Spence."

Christine snapped her fingers. "Michelle doesn't like being less than perfect, either. Didn't the person in the bathroom complain because she had paint on her fingers?"

Meredith wrote Michelle V. Hagen on the sheet of notebook paper. "Heather Linton and Julie Anderson are Corrin's best friends," she said.

Christine crinkled her nose. "Would one of them want to hurt her?"

"Maybe, if they were secretly jealous or mad. Plus, since they're close to her, they'd know what really upsets her."

"Okay." Nicki pointed to the paper. "I guess you should write them down, too."

"We know Kim didn't do it," Laura said. "Meredith, can we be sure *you* didn't do it?"

Meredith dropped her jaw. "What?"

"You and Corrin had that big run-in last year. I'm just making sure you don't have it in for her."

Meredith's eyes flashed. "If Corrin Burns gets into trouble, it'll be because of her own big mouth, not anything I did. I didn't do anything to her."

"Meredith didn't have an opportunity, either," Chris said, watching with a half-smile. "She was with us when Scott's locker was painted."

Laura nodded. "You're right."

Nicki tilted her head. "You know, there's another name we ought to add to the list. Write Corrin Burns's name on your paper."

Christine made a face. "Why would Corrin steal her own paper and paint her own locker?"

"Why would she pick on Scott Spence when she practically drools on the guy every time he walks by?" Laura asked.

Nicki shrugged. "I don't know. But Meredith said that Corrin's troubles might spring from her own big mouth, and that's certainly true. Plus she's a girl, plus she had opportunity—"

"To steal her own paper?" Laura said.

"Sure. She got an extra two days to finish it, didn't she? Just add her name to the list."

By the time the limo driver pulled up outside Christine's house, the list of suspects included:

| Name: | Motive: | Opportunity: |
| --- | --- | --- |
| Michelle V. Hagen | jealousy? | yes/maybe |
| Heather Linton | ? | yes/maybe |
| Julie Anderson | ? | yes/maybe |
| Corrin Burns | attention? | yes/maybe |

# Eleven

Nicki found Scott Spence leaning against her locker on Monday morning. The guy flashed a smile as wide as Texas.

"Hey, Scott. Did Mack come home?"

He grinned. "Yesterday."

Nicki opened her locker. "I told you he got out somehow."

Scott shook his head. "I don't think so."

"Why not?"

Scott's smile faded. "When Mack came home, he was wearing this around his neck." He pulled a bright yellow kerchief from his jacket pocket. Someone had inked the mystery mark on the cotton material.

Nicki took the kerchief and held it up. "What is this about?"

"Wow," Meredith said as she, Christine, Kim, and Laura walked up. "Did you find that in your locker, Scott?"

"It was around Mack's neck when he finally came home."

Christine hugged her books to her chest. "Was he hurt? Please tell us he wasn't hurt."

"He was fine." Scott gave her a smile. "Whoever took Mack took good care of him as far as I can tell. But why would anyone take him at all? He's not an easy dog to take care of. He eats four or five times as much as other dogs. And if someone had him inside the house, well—" He grinned. "Let's just say he eats coffee tables for breakfast."

"Would serve our dognapper right if they got in trouble,"

Nicki said, fingering the kerchief. "Someone is definitely sending you a message, though. And how did they get this symbol on this cotton material? This isn't paint. It looks more like India ink."

"What's India ink?" Scott asked.

"It's a special ink that won't run if it gets wet," Nicki explained. "Usually it's sold in bottles. To use it you have to dip an old-fashioned pen into the ink—you know, like Ben Franklin used to. My music teacher makes me write my compositions with it. It's permanent dye, and it can make a real mess."

"That is how they make the figures so perfectly," Kim said. "It is hard to write in Chinese or Korean with a ballpoint pen. Oriental figures are thin in some places, thick in others."

"There's one way to test it." Meredith took the kerchief from Nicki and walked to the water fountain. She wet the material, then rubbed the inked lines together. "It's not running," she called. "It must be India ink—or something like it."

"Wait a minute." Nicki fumbled through her notebook and took out a yellow sheet of paper. "This is the page Mr. Cardoza gave us—the one Corrin found in her locker." Nicki walked to the water fountain and splashed a few drops on the black wri ting.

"That's India ink, too," she said, smiling. "It isn't running, either."

"So our culprit writes with an old-fashioned pen dipped in India ink," Christine said.

"Who could that be?" Laura asked. "Are we looking for a musician or an artist?"

"It could still be anyone," Nicki said, drying the yellow paper with a dry edge of the kerchief. "You can buy the pens at any stationery store, and India ink isn't hard to find, either." She smiled at Scott. "But at least Mack's back and you don't have to worry about him being turned into a dog burger."

Scott laughed. "Yeah, that's a relief. And you can keep the kerchief. Right now I'd do anything to help you catch whoever is behind all this."

Nicki grinned. "Well, there's a place we have to investigate now, and I don't think you'll want to come."

Scott lifted a brow. "Where?"

Christine giggled. "I think I know—the girls' water closet!"

—

Meredith held her nose as Christine dug through the trash in the girls' rest room. "Do you know what kinds of germs are in there?"

"This can't be any worse than cleaning my brother's room," Christine said, pulling wet paper towels off her freckled arms. "I've had to do it for a month now."

Nicki laughed. "What did you do this time?"

"Not much." Christine went to the sink and turned on the water. "I sprayed him with a can of shaving cream while his date was waiting in the living room." She giggled. "It was worth it. He deserved it after calling me—well, that name."

Laura's eyes went wide. "What name did he call you?"

"Promise you'll never call me that?"

"Sure." All the girls nodded.

"Christine Listerine. For that he deserved a face full of shaving cream."

As Nicki and Laura laughed, Meredith leaned against the wall and crossed her arms. "There's nothing here. The custodian must have cleaned up over the weekend."

Nicki stared at the sink. "If you had paint on your fingers, what would you do?"

"Wash my hands," Kim said. "Whoever was speaking was standing by the sink. I heard water running."

Nicki touched the rim of the sink. "There's nothing to see here," she said. "No smudges, no fingerprints, nothing that can help us."

Just then the door opened and Michelle Vander Hagen walked in. "Oh—" She stopped in her tracks. "Hi. You girls aren't smoking in here, are you?"

Nicki frowned. "We're just talking."

"Good," Michelle answered. "I heard just *breathing* someone else's smoke will give you wrinkles." Michelle walked to the mirror, gave the mirror a practice smile, and wiped a smudge of lip gloss from her front teeth. Her eyes darted over the rim of the sink.

Christine stepped forward. "Lose something, Michelle?"

"No. Just wanted to make sure you all were telling the truth. I'd hate to smell like cigarette smoke all day long."

Michelle turned on her heel and left. When the door had

closed, Christine crossed her arms. "Of all the nerve! Why would she think we were smoking?"

"What if Michelle came in here for the same reasons we did?" Meredith asked. "What if she was making sure she didn't leave any fingerprints, smudges, or paint cans?"

Nicki bit her lip. "What if?"

# Twelve

At lunch Nicki decided to be totally honest with Kim.

"At first, Kim," she began, "we thought you might have something to do with what's been going on in school. But when Scott's dog was stolen and you were with us, we knew you couldn't be involved."

Kim looked down at her lunch tray. "Why would you think of me?"

Christine cracked open her milk carton. "The yellow papers. Your locker was full of them and you said they were yours. Why did you say that?"

Kim shook her head. "They were in my locker. I supposed someone had given them to me. That would make them mine, would it not?"

Meredith waved a plastic fork in Kim's direction. "But how could someone put them in your locker? Does someone have your locker combination?"

Laura smiled. "I know how they did it. They had all been folded small enough that someone could have slid them into Kim's locker through the vents in the door. They were all on top of her things, remember? When she opened the door, half of them fell out."

Christine shook her finger at her friends. "She's right. Someone stuffed Kim's locker full of yellow papers so we'd *think* she did it. And we fell for it—for a little while, anyway."

"That paper Scott found in his locker was folded, too," Nicki said. "And so was the one you found in your book bag, right, Meredith?"

Meredith nodded. "But all that means is that someone had to get the paper small enough to fit either in a locker or in my book bag. Anyone could have folded a paper."

"But who would want to?" Nicki asked. "And who would want to take Scott's dog?" She stirred her milk slowly. "Meredith, do you still have our list of suspects?"

Meredith nodded and pulled the list from her notebook. "Michelle Vander Hagen," she read. "Could she have planted the papers in Scott's and Kim's lockers?"

The other girls nodded.

"Could she have taken Scott's dog?"

"She does live in the same neighborhood," Christine pointed out. "But so does Corrin. And so do Nicki and I, for that matter."

"Me, too," said Meredith. "At least during the week."

Nicki glanced at the list. "Okay, let's try something else. Could Michelle have stolen Corrin's paper?"

"Practically anyone could steal anyone's paper anytime," Christine said. "Just look at the benches out in the courtyard. There are at least fifty notebooks out there now, and there are probably ninety others scattered all over the place before the morning bell rings."

Laura shrugged. "Who guards their notebook? It's silly to steal someone's homework unless it's something like a math paper. It would be too easy to recognize the handwriting."

Meredith squealed. "That's it! I know where we may find a big clue!"

Christine stared. "What are you talking about?"

The bell rang. "You'll see next period in English," Meredith said, picking up her books.

———

Mr. Cardoza cleared his throat and put down his attendance roster. "Class, please take out your reading books and turn to page 67," he said.

Meredith raised her hand. "Mr. Cardoza, did you grade my research paper over the weekend?"

"Oh yes." Mr. Cardoza leaned over his desk. "I have two papers to return to the owners." He peered over the top of his reading glasses. "I thought it was interesting that both papers were on Shakespeare."

Nicki bit her tongue to keep from shouting. So that's what Meredith meant! Corrin must have taken Meredith's paper and copied it!

Meredith had the same idea. "Mr. Cardoza," she said, glancing at Corrin, "were they both on Shakespeare's *Hamlet*?"

"Actually, no." Mr. Cardoza's voice deepened. "Miss Burns's paper was on *Romeo and Juliet*. It was excellent and earned an A."

Meredith's jaw dropped as Mr. Cardoza handed a neatly

typed report to Corrin, who smiled and cast a "ha-ha" look in Meredith's direction.

"Your paper, Miss Dixon, was not up to your usual fine standards." Mr. Cardoza frowned and looked at the report Meredith had written in a hurry. "You had good thoughts here, but when I compared it to Miss Burns's paper, I felt I could not give it an A."

Meredith's paper had a B+ written on the cover. She accepted the paper, but she looked like she was about to throw up.

"My first B," she whispered to Nicki. "What will I tell my parents?"

"How could Corrin write an A paper?" Christine whispered. "Especially on *Romeo and Juliet*?"

Laura snickered. "Maybe she watched the movie."

"I'm sure she didn't read the play," Meredith said. "It took me two solid weeks to read *Hamlet*. Half the time I was reading footnotes just to figure out what they were saying."

Laura's eyes opened wide. "Maybe it's the curse."

"It's no curse," Nicki answered, her voice flat. "Somebody's up to something and we've got to figure this out!"

"If we don't," Meredith said, still looking queasy, "I may never earn another A in my life!"

Nicki was glad to hear that Mr. Padgett had scheduled a student body meeting for sixth period. The principal stood in the gym and waited for the movement in the bleachers to stop. When everyone stopped talking, he picked up a microphone.

"As you know"—his voice screeched over the microphone—"each October we have a Fall Festival here at Pine Grove Middle School. As part of the festivities, we elect royal representatives from the student body. Seventh and eighth graders are eligible as long as they have a C+ average. We will take nominations in homeroom next week."

Christine elbowed Nicki and nodded in Michelle Vander Hagen's direction. Michelle had bowed her head modestly when Mr. Padgett mentioned the elections and now she was smiling as if she had already won.

"What we need from you is an idea," Mr. Padgett went on. "Last year we had a harvest dance and the year before that we celebrated with a harvest hayride. I'm still getting hay out of my clothes from that event."

The teachers chuckled while the students groaned.

"If you have an idea or suggestion, pass it on to me or your homeroom teacher. Thank you for your attention and have a good afternoon."

The teachers dismissed them, and the girls stood up in the bleachers. "I have to go quickly," Kim said, pulling a stray piece of hair behind her ear. "My mother is not well and I have to baby-sit for a neighbor today. I will see you tomorrow."

Nicki watched her newest friend walk down the bleachers. "I wish we could do something to help her. Kim isn't baby-sitting to earn spending money, you know. I think she's trying to help her dad earn money for her mother's operation."

Christine shrugged. "What can we do? We're not made of money."

Every head turned toward Laura. "Um, I'm not made of money, either," she said, crossing her arms. "My mother is."

Meredith dropped her loaded book bag onto a bench. "I'm not sure Kim's parents would take money if you just handed it to them. Some people are too proud to accept money from strangers."

"But can we help?" Nicki asked. "Surely there's something we can do."

Christine started moving down the bleachers. "Hey, you guys, can we stop in the locker room before we go home? I left my jacket in my gym locker."

The four girls climbed down from the bleachers, then walked into the darkened girls' locker room. Nicki shuddered. "This place is kind of spooky with the lights off."

"Nothing to worry about," Christine said. "I kind of like it like this." Looking at the others, she moved to her locker and groped for the handle. "All you need is one week in a house with six kids and you'd like peace and quiet, too."

Nicki heard a metallic squeak as the locker door opened. "Hey," Chris said, groping in the compartment. "My jacket's not in here. My gym clothes are, but what's this?" She pulled out a small bottle. The label read India Ink.

Nicki gasped. "That's not your locker, Christine. Yours isn't forty-eight, it's fifty-eight. So whose locker is that?"

One row over, Meredith opened locker fifty-eight and pulled out Christine's denim jacket. Christine pulled a sweatshirt from locker forty-eight and looked for a name. "I've found it," she said, holding the name tag up to the thin beam of light from the P.E. teacher's office. "You won't believe whose locker this is."

"Whose?"

"Michelle Vander Hagen's."

# Thirteen

The next morning, Nicki, Laura, Christine, and Meredith sat in chairs outside Mr. Padgett's office. Christine sat on her hands and let her legs swing back and forth. "This is the first time I've ever been to the principal's office for something good. He'll be surprised to see me."

"Do you think we'll be heroes?" Laura asked.

Nicki laughed. "We ought to be."

Mr. Padgett finally opened his door. "Come on in, girls."

The girls filed in and sat on a couch against the wall. The principal sat in a chair across from them. "Is this a casual visit?" he asked. "Or can I help you girls with something?"

"We're here for two reasons," Nicki said. "First, we have an idea for the Fall Festival."

The principal's eyes sparkled with interest. "I'm listening."

Nicki grinned at the others, then drew a deep breath. "Why not have a Fall Festival Fun Fair with games, a dunking booth, a cakewalk, and maybe a craft sale? There are lots of people in town who would like to sell their crafts. But the most important part is that the admission charge and money from the school exhibits would be donated to a fund for Mrs. Park's kidney transplant."

"We know the Parks may not accept charity from strangers," Laura explained, "but this wouldn't be charity, not exactly. We'd earn it, and Kim could help us."

Meredith chimed in. "You could crown the Fall Festival queen and king at the fair. Every kid in school and their parents would come out for that."

"The band could play—"

"The choir could sing—"

"And the shop students could make booths."

Mr. Padgett smiled. "Well," he said, rubbing his chin, "I think that's a great idea. Could we pull it off in three weeks?"

Nicki nodded. "I think we can, especially since we've found the person who has been painting lockers and causing trouble."

Mr. Padgett's brows lifted. "Who?"

"We found a bottle of India ink in Michelle Vander Hagen's locker," Meredith said. "We didn't mean to snoop, but we know the same person who painted the lockers also drew that strange symbol on yellow papers with India ink."

"We think Michelle hid the ink in her gym locker because nobody ever looks through dirty gym clothes," Nicki added.

Mr. Padgett closed his eyes. "Why would Michelle do that?"

The girls looked at each other. "We're not exactly sure," Nicki said, "but we think she's jealous of any girl who flirts with Scott Spence. That's why she painted Corrin's locker."

"But another locker was painted, too," Mr. Padgett pointed out.

Nicki nodded. "We think she painted Scott's locker because a rumor got around school that Scott likes Kim Park. So Michelle was mad at Scott, too."

The principal put his finger across his lips while he thought, then he turned to Meredith. "Mr. Cardoza mentioned that you had a paper stolen. Is that true?"

Meredith nodded.

"Why would Michelle steal one of your papers? Were you flirting with Scott, too?"

Meredith looked at Nicki for help. "At first I thought Corrin took my paper on Shakespeare and copied it," she said. "But then I found out Corrin did her paper on another play. I don't know why Michelle would take my paper, but I'm friendly with Kim, and whoever is doing this is mad at Kim, too . . ."

"Why?" the principal asked.

Laura leaned forward. "Jealousy. You don't know what a jealous woman will do! In *Jane Eyre*, a crazy woman ripped up Jane's wedding veil and burned down the house! There's no predicting the actions of a woman mad with jealousy!"

Mr. Padgett smiled, then nodded and stood. "Thank you, girls, for coming in to see me. I'll call Michelle in later today and discuss these things with her. If I were you, I'd keep my suspicions to myself for now. Here at Pine Grove, someone is innocent until proven guilty."

Laura sputtered. "But the ink—"

"—is only circumstantial evidence," Mr. Padgett said. He patted Nicki on the back. "But your idea for a Fall Festival Fun Fair is terrific. Let's go for it!"

—

"Christine, can your father announce the fair at the Christian school?" Nicki asked at lunch. Since Mr. Kelshaw's school only enrolled first through fifth graders, the fair was a natural for them. "I'll bet the little kids would love it."

Christine nodded. "Sure. We can have it announced at my church, too. Some of our people know the Parks. They have been visiting Kim's family."

Kim smiled. "My father likes the Christians. We are Buddhist, but the Christians have been kind to us."

"I can handle the publicity," Meredith offered. "My parents can have some posters printed up for us at the university printing office. It won't cost much at all."

"My parents know a lot of people in business," Nicki said. "I'll be in charge of signing up merchants to fill the booths."

Laura grinned. "I think I can talk my mother into loaning our car for the king and queen to ride in. She'll probably want to make a donation, too."

Kim raised her hand. "What can I do?"

"You can take care of your mother and let your parents know we really want to help," Nicki said. "Try to talk your father into coming to the fair to pick up the money we raise for your mom's operation."

She stopped talking when Michelle Vander Hagen walked up to the table. Her brown eyes snapped with anger and her nose and eyes were red. "Nicki Holland and company, I hate you!"

Heads turned from every direction. Nicki nearly choked on her hamburger.

But Michelle was just getting started. "How *dare* you accuse me to the principal! You were wrong! Who gave you the right to snoop around and accuse perfectly innocent people of stupid things like painting lockers? Who made you the great investigator?" Michelle stood at the end of the table, gulping for breath. Nicki could see that the girl was dead serious and furious.

Nicki looked at Meredith, then tried to explain. "I'm sorry, Michelle, but we found the India ink accidentally."

"I don't care what you did, Nicki." Michelle raised her chin and looked down on them. "That stupid bottle of ink wasn't mine. Someone must have stashed it in my locker. You were wrong and you're a snoop and I don't care who knows it."

Michelle spun on her heel and left. Nicki and her friends stared at each other.

Laura looked like she was about to cry. "I can't stand this. I feel horrible. I think she's telling the truth."

Nicki looked down at her lunch and realized she had lost her appetite. "I don't feel too great myself. I think we jumped to conclusions."

"We didn't have all the facts," Meredith said. "And we knew better."

"I think we need to apologize," Christine said. "Although Michelle may never speak to us again."

"Half the school may never speak to us again," Meredith added, looking around. "Everyone heard Michelle. They all probably think we're either nosy or nuts."

"Including the real culprit," Nicki pointed out. "Somebody fooled us good."

"I don't care," Laura wailed. "I'm afraid to go around looking for clues. What happens if we accuse the wrong person again?"

Nicki shook her head. "We can't give up. We'll just have to keep quiet until we're absolutely sure. Until we have proof."

# Fourteen

The next two weeks passed in a rush. The girls worked hard on the Fall Festival Fun Fair, partly, Nicki realized, because they wanted to prove to their classmates that they weren't the traitors, snoops, and awful human beings Michelle said they were. Laura worked especially hard and Nicki noticed that she was beginning to make friends everywhere.

Nicki tried to apologize to Michelle, but got only a stony glance in response. But on the Monday morning when the students voted for the seventh grade's Fall Festival king and queen, Michelle's iciness finally thawed.

"I forgive you, okay?" she told Nicki and her friends in homeroom. "I wouldn't want there to be anymore hard feelings. Everyone knows now that I didn't do those weird things."

Mrs. Balian handed out the nomination forms. "Write in the name of the guy and girl you feel would be the best seventh-grade king and queen," she instructed. "After the votes are counted, the top five will have their grade point averages evaluated by the teachers and the principal. The young man and woman with the highest grade point averages will be our Fall Festival royal representatives."

Nicki looked at her nomination form. Who would make a good queen? She glanced around the room. Michelle was beautiful, no doubt about it. She had not hesitated a minute and was busy writing in her choice for queen—*herself, surely*.

But even though she was the prettiest girl in school, Michelle was so distant Nicki doubted if she had any good girl friends.

Corrin Burns could be a real pain if you weren't one of her "kind," but she was known around school as being a lot of fun. She had many friends, although all of them were white, middle-class kids who dressed, walked, and talked just like Corrin.

Meredith was smart, probably the smartest kid to come through Pine Grove Middle in twenty years, but most kids didn't relate to her very well. Christine was funny and mischievous, but too goofy to be royal. Kim was cute and smart, but she was still shy around people she didn't know. Aside from Nicki and her friends, Kim was a mystery to everyone else at Pine Grove.

What about Laura? Nicki looked at her as she bent over her own nomination form. Laura was sweet, gentle, pretty, rich, sophisticated, and poised—plus she made good grades. In the last few weeks she had left the security of her circle and made new friends, too. What better choice could there be?

Nicki wrote "Laura Cushman" on her form, then she folded it and waited for Mrs. Balian to collect them.

—

In the seventh-grade class meeting that afternoon, Mr. Padgett didn't even have to wait to get everyone's attention. Eager to hear the results of the election, the crowd quieted as soon as he picked up the microphone.

"I'd like to announce our Fall Festival representatives," he said, his voice echoing in the unusual stillness. "But first, Mrs. Balian will make some announcements about this weekend's activities."

A groan rumbled through the bleachers as Mrs. Balian took the mic from the principal's hand. "We want you to let your families know what will be going on next Friday and Saturday at the festival," she said. "The games, booths, and kiddie rides will open at 4:00 PM on Friday and 10:00 AM on Saturday. Food vendors will serve hot dogs and hamburgers all day, so come prepared to eat!

"Band and choir members should be here at the school at 6:00 PM Friday for the miniparade from the school to the fairgrounds," she continued. "Our marching band will begin the parade, the choir float will follow, and the car for our royalty will bring up the rear."

"So who won?" someone called from the crowd.

Mrs. Balian frowned at the interruption. "After the parade has arrived at the fairgrounds, the seventh-grade king and queen will be crowned. Door prizes, which were graciously donated by area merchants, will then be awarded and presented by our queen. Make sure you and your parents are present. It's going to be a fun evening for everyone."

Mrs. Balian sat down. Mr. Padgett took the microphone from her. "Would you like to hear the names of our royalty?" he asked.

"Yes!" the seventh graders roared.

"The eighth-grade representatives were announced earlier today in their class meeting," Mr. Padgett said. "Anne Taylor and Mark Todd. They will be crowned at the fair on Saturday night."

Mr. Padgett obviously enjoyed keeping them in suspense. "First runner-up for king is Jeff Jordan," he finally said, his voice booming. "First runner-up for queen is Corrin Burns."

Nicki could see Corrin's friends buzzing. Twenty or thirty hands were slapping Jeff on the back. "If the seventh-grade representatives are unable to attend, these runner-ups will step in," Mr. Padgett said.

"Are you ready?" the principal called. Nicki could see Michelle Vander Hagen straighten. Corrin slumped, looking defeated.

"Our Fall Festival king will be . . . Scott Spence!" The crowd roared and Scott, who was sitting next to Jeff Jordan, grinned.

"Our Fall Festival queen will be . . . Laura Cushman!" Nicki heard a gasp of surprise from the crowd. Laughing, she turned to her friend. "Laura, that's great news!"

Laura's eyes were wide and her mouth open in a most un-Laura-like expression. "Wh-what?"

"You and Scott Spence!" Christine squealed, her face as red as her hair. "Can you get any luckier?"

"Way to go, Laura," Meredith said. "You'll show them that brains and beauty can go together."

"Congratulations," Kim said, smiling. "You will make a good queen."

Everyone within five bleachers rose up to congratulate Laura, including Heather Linton and Julie Anderson. Nicki looked through the crowd for Michelle Vander Hagen, but she had disappeared. So, Nicki noticed, had Corrin Burns.

◆

Instead of having her driver drop her off at Nicki's as she usually did, Laura asked him to pick up all the girls the next morning so they could ride to school in style. "I figured we could celebrate," she said, blushing.

"It's okay, your highness," Christine said, bowing her head. "We are your humble servants."

Laura laughed. "Oh, cut it out."

"What will Michelle Vander Hagen do now?" Meredith wanted to know. "I had the feeling she was living for the chance to be festival queen."

"She'll survive," Nicki said, gathering her books as the car pulled up at the school. "She'll tell us she's auditioning for Miss America or something."

◆

Apparently Michelle had recovered. "Congratulations, Laura," she called, smiling as she came into homeroom. "But you know, I think it's more important to be festival queen in the eighth grade than the seventh, don't you?"

Laura gave her a polite smile. "Thank you, but I wouldn't know. I've never been a queen."

Nicki leaned toward her friend. "Don't let her get to you," she whispered. "She's already planning her strategy for next year."

Scott Spence grinned and leaned over his desk. "Hey, Nick! So there's royalty in your group now."

Nicki laughed as Laura turned the color of her tomato-red sweater. "You'd better watch it, your majesty," she called. "If you abuse your position, the peasants may overthrow you."

"What we need, sire," Meredith said, inclining her head in Scott's direction, "is a little royal manpower. Can you get some of your servants and meet us at the fairgrounds after school on Thursday? We've got to help put up booths and the platform."

"Consider it done," Scott said, sending a salute in Meredith's direction.

Scott and several of his friends did show up Thursday after school to help work at the fairgrounds. The shop teacher and the art teacher had built frames for the booths, and now it was the students' job to assemble them. Everyone worked hard, and when it was all done, they were proud of their work.

Mr. Spence showed up at dinnertime and brought soft drinks for everyone. "It looks great," Christine told Nicki as the girls rested on the large platform for the crowning of the king and queen. "Just think, it was all our idea. The fair will earn lots of money for Mrs. Park's operation, and everyone will have fun, too."

"Best of all," Meredith said, "our good friend will be festival queen. When I think that Corrin almost won—"

"But she didn't," Nicki said. "So why spoil a beautiful afternoon thinking like that?"

They laughed and Nicki leaned back on her elbows to look over the fairgrounds once again. Everything looked great and Nicki knew the place would look even better when the merchants had filled the booths and people had filled the park. She looked once again at the banner that fluttered in the breeze and proudly proclaimed, "PGMS Presents the Fall Festival Fun Fair."

She blinked. "Ohmigoodness, what's that?"

Meredith looked at her. "What?"

"That yellow thing hanging from the banner."

The girls turned, and there it was—a yellow square hanging from the lower corner of the banner. "I'll go get it," Christine volunteered. She jumped from the platform and sprinted toward the banner.

She brought back a yellow paper folded twice. The outside was marked "Laura Cushman."

Nicki pointed to the note. "Look at those letters. Remind you of anything?"

Christine nodded. "It's the same style of writing on the paper in Scott's locker."

"The note that said 'DOG MEAT,' " Meredith added.

Nicki handed the paper to Laura. "I guess you should open it."

Laura's hand trembled as she unfolded the page. "I don't want to hear anything about this curse stuff." She tried to laugh when she saw what was on the paper—the mystery mark and two words: STAY HOME.

# Fifteen

"Wow, Laura, you look pale," Christine said. "You're not scared, are you? You can't really believe in this curse stuff."

Nicki rose to her friend's defense. "Of course she doesn't." But Laura's eyes were wide and her hands were twisting her necklace . . .

"This is different," Laura said, her voice weak. "Meredith and Corrin lost their papers and Scott lost his dog, but what if someone tries something really serious tomorrow night?"

Christine put her arm through Laura's. "Relax."

"Easy for you to say," Laura said.

Nicki took the yellow paper and studied it. It was the same mystery mark drawn in the same ink. "Who could have done this?"

"Who'd be mad at Laura for winning?" Christine asked. "Maybe we were wrong when we apologized to Michelle Vander Hagen. Maybe she's really a terrific actress and turned on the tears so we'd feel bad and leave her alone. She didn't want Laura to win! Michelle was all ready to be queen, but Laura snatched that crown right off her head."

"I didn't want to," Laura said, giving Nicki a weak smile. "She can have it back."

"Oh no." Meredith pounded her on the back. "You're not going to give up. You're made of strong stuff."

"Remember Scarlett O'Hara from *Gone With the Wind*?" Nicki

said. "She was from Georgia, just like you, and nothing scared her. You southern belles are tough!"

"Tough as nails," Christine said.

Laura blew out a breath. "Right now I feel more like Play-Doh."

"I wouldn't worry," Meredith said. "If Michelle couldn't win, she was going to make sure Laura didn't enjoy winning. She only wanted to scare you. She wouldn't actually *do* anything."

"I wouldn't be too sure," Laura said. "I think I would almost rather stay home than come, but my mother would kill me. She brought in an Atlanta designer to make my dress."

Christine shook her head. "I can't remember the last time I had a new dress. My clothes are all from my sister. I'm only grateful that Torrie has pretty good taste." She glanced down at her jeans and T-shirt. "This *is* okay, isn't it?"

"You look fine," Nicki said. "But let's get back to this note. How'd it get on the banner? Were any of our suspects around today?"

Christine crossed her arms. "People have been out here all day. The art class came before lunch and hung the banner. The shop classes came after lunch and dropped off the platform and the frames for the booths. There have been people in and out and about—"

"Michelle is in the art class," Meredith pointed out.

"And Heather, Julie, and Corrin are in the choir," Kim said. "They brought their float out after lunch."

Nicki sighed. "Okay, so any of our suspects could have done it. But this time I'm not going to make any accusations until we know *for sure* who the guilty party is. There are still people at school who look at me strangely since that little episode with Michelle. If there's one thing I don't need, it's a reputation as a troublemaker."

"That's probably the last thing you'll ever have," Meredith said, smiling.

Laura lifted her head. "Okay, I'll go through with everything. I guess I can be as tough as nails."

"Good!" Nicki said.

"Just promise me one thing."

"What?"

Laura's shoulders drooped. "Please, please, will all of you ride in the limo with me and Scott? You can be the queen's ladies-in-waiting."

The girls looked at each other, then Christine let out a whoop.

"You're my best friends," Laura said. "I need you for support. I feel safer with all of you around."

Nicki could hardly sit still in class on Friday morning. "I don't think I'm going to be able to study today at all!" she whispered to Christine.

The redhead grinned. "I know. Torrie helped me pick out a really nice dress to wear tonight and she's going to put a French braid in my hair."

"I don't know if you'll have time for that," Laura said. "I told Mrs. Balian y'all were going to be my ladies-in-waiting and she suggested we have our pictures taken after school for the yearbook. I'm having the limo driver bring my dress to school so I can change here. If you like, I can have him pick up your dresses, too."

"That'd be great!"

Laura turned to Kim. "Kim, my mom wanted to get you something special in honor of your family. The driver is bringing a new dress for you, too."

Kim blushed and bowed her head. "*Kamsamnida* is the Korean word for 'Thank you,' " she said. "Thank your kind mother for me."

"Kam-sahm-nee-da," Nicki whispered. Her first word in Korean.

Mr. Padgett's voice boomed over the intercom and interrupted the morning quiet. "Mrs. Balian, would you please send Nicki Holland to the office?"

"Certainly," she replied.

"And you may count both Michelle Vander Hagen and Corrin Burns present," the principal continued. "They are here in the office."

"Thank you." Mrs. Balian looked at Nicki. "I suppose you'd better go now."

Christine leaned forward. "What's going on? Do you think Mr. Padgett solved the mystery?"

Nicki gathered her books. "I don't know, but I'll tell you what's up later. See you in science class."

---

Mr. Padgett's secretary looked up and nodded briskly at Nicki. "The principal is waiting in his office for you."

Nicki knocked on his door. "Come in," he said.

In Mr. Padgett's office were Corrin and Michelle. Michelle glared at Nicki. If looks could kill . . .

Nicki took a seat facing the principal.

"Nicki," he began, "I think we should talk."

"Good," Nicki answered. "There's something you should know. Laura Cushman found one of those mystery marks yesterday, and the note threatened her. She was almost afraid"—Nicki looked at Michelle—"to be crowned festival queen, but we talked her into going through with everything."

"Where did Laura find this note?"

"Actually, I found it," Nicki answered. "I saw it hanging from the banner at the fairgrounds."

"Very convenient," Corrin snapped. "You saw the note and made *real* sure Laura saw it, didn't you?"

Nicki stared at the other girl. "What are you saying?"

"Nicki," Mr. Padgett said, "these girls have brought proof to indicate that you are the guilty party in this little brouhaha. Corrin, show her what you've brought."

Corrin pulled several sheets of crumpled typing paper from

her book bag. "This is Meredith Dixon's English paper," she said, practically snarling at Nicki. "I found it when I was helping Mr. Bracken clean up the science lab. It was in the cabinet next to your desk, Nicki Holland!"

The principal looked at her. "Did you take Meredith's report, Nicki?"

"No, sir!"

Corrin's face went red. "But she had the gall to say *I* did! Meredith even asked Mr. Cardoza, in front of everybody, if my paper was like hers. But it wasn't. And my paper got an A."

Mr. Padgett looked at Michelle. "Do you have something to say?"

Michelle raised her chin. "At first I was just mad because Nicki and her friends accused *me* of doing these nasty things. But then I thought maybe *she* was the one who put that India ink stuff in my locker. And as I thought more about it, I wondered who in the world would even know what that ink was, except the person who had used it? *I'd* never heard of it. And then I realized that every time something has happened, Nicki Holland has been right there on the spot. I mean, don't you think that's, like, amazingly coincidental?"

Again the principal looked at Nicki. "What would you like to say about this?"

Nicki shook her head. "I can't believe this. I didn't do any of these things. I'm trying to solve the mystery, not cause it."

"You're trying to *cause* it because you want to convince everyone you're some kind of great detective," Michelle said. "Well, it's not going to work. We know what you're doing."

"That's enough, girls," Mr. Padgett said. "I haven't exactly figured this out, but I do know that as long as there is a reasonable doubt, Nicki, I can't allow you to participate in the fair. Since the festival was your idea, I was going to ask you to present the check to Mr. and Mrs. Park, but now that may not be appropriate."

He looked at the other two girls. "I don't know who is behind all this foolishness," he said, his voice stern, "but I have a hunch the problem lies with someone in this room. So I'll warn all three of you—stay away from Laura Cushman."

—

In less than an hour, the entire school had heard that Nicki was in some kind of trouble, and even her best friends were avoiding her. Michelle and Corrin were saying that Nicki was a thief, a snob, and boy-crazy.

"Imagine," Michelle told a group of girls, "she was so crazy over Scott Spence that she stole his dog just so she could go over there and 'investigate.' "

The rumors flew thick and fast. Kids who saw Nicki sitting at one table and her friends at another thought she was really Out. But they didn't know she was Out because she had asked to be.

"Come on, Nicki," Laura had begged. "We don't believe a word of that story."

"It isn't even logical," Meredith pointed out. "Even if your motive was genuine, you didn't have the opportunity to commit the crimes."

Christine glared at Meredith. "I don't care if you had motive and opportunity. I know you, Nick, and I won't believe a word of it. You're our friend and we believe in you. Come on and sit with us."

Nicki shook her head. "Mr. Padgett wants me to stay away from Laura, and I don't want him to think I'm disobeying on purpose."

"I'll sit by myself," Laura offered.

Nicki shook her head again. "That's okay, but that wouldn't be fair. I'll be fine. This will all be straightened out soon and things will be back to normal."

But Kim Park was unswervingly loyal. When Nicki put her tray down on an empty table, Kim followed and sat across from her.

"Kim, you should sit with the others," Nicki said. "It's okay. Michelle and Corrin aren't going to get the best of me."

Kim crossed her arms. "I am being a friend. Some people from Christine's church came to visit my mother. They read a beautiful poem about friendship."

Kim closed her eyes and began to speak in an older woman's voice: "Love is never glad about injustice, but rejoices whenever truth wins out. If you love someone, you will be loyal to him no matter what the cost. You will always believe in him, always expect the best of him, and always stand your ground in defending him."

Her eyelids fluttered open. "If that is not a poem about friendship, what is?"

Nicki smiled. "I think that's from the Bible."

"The Bible is a book about friends?"

"You could say that." Nicki glanced to the nearest table, where Julie and Heather were looking at her and whispering. "Look, Kim, word is that I'm a stuck-up troublemaker. If you sit here, everyone will think you're stuck-up, too."

"That is okay by me," Kim said. She opened her mouth: "Get outta here, you little Chink."

Nicki stared. Kim had spoken in the unmistakable tones of Corrin.

"Where did you hear that?"

Kim opened her mouth again: "My father says you Japs are buying up this country. I don't think we want you around here." This time Kim spoke in Michelle's voice.

Nicki shook her head. "Michelle said that?"

Kim nodded. "I could do others, but I would prefer to sit here by my 'stuck-up' friend."

# Sixteen

Nicki and Kim sat on a bench in the courtyard after school and watched Meredith, Christine, and Laura head toward the girls' rest room to do their hair for the yearbook pictures. "You should go, too," Nicki told Kim. "Laura wants you to be part of her court."

Kim didn't move, but spoke in a voice not her own: "If rain falls in the garden of my friend, I get wet."

Nicki grinned. "That's nice. Who said it?"

"My mother."

Nicki leaned forward and rested her chin on her hands. "Right now the sun is shining on the garden of my friends, but I'm not exactly getting a sunburn." She closed her eyes. "I wish we could solve this mystery. It's driving me crazy."

"We could," Kim said. "We could think harder."

Nicki opened her eyes. "Let's think back to the scene of the first crime. Corrin ran into class and said her report had been stolen from her locker."

"She said the locker had been open about ten minutes," Kim added.

Nicki nodded. "So apparently our culprit took the report during that time. But Corrin said she closed the locker and went to homeroom without noticing anything unusual. But when she came to English class . . ." Nicki paused and pushed the backs of her hands against her forehead, trying to remember. "When she came to English she was carrying the yellow paper with the mystery mark on it."

Kim nodded. "She said she found it in her locker."

"So the culprit must have put the paper in her locker *after* she locked it again. Just like the criminal filled your locker with papers and left a note for Scott."

"Little folded papers." Kim shook her head. "I was new then. I did not know what to think of them."

"You were being framed." Nicki sighed. "There was a paper in Scott's locker, a paper in Meredith's book bag, a yellow paper hanging from the banner yesterday . . ." She gazed off into the distance, then remembered. "I have those papers." She opened her notebook and pulled out the pages. "Is there a clue in this collection?"

Kim looked at the four yellow papers. "There is little difference in the mystery marks," she said. "All are written in India ink. Scott's paper says DOG MEAT—"

"Another attempt to frame you."

"—and Laura's paper says STAY HOME."

"A direct warning to Laura."

Kim shrugged. "There is only one difference."

"What's that?"

"This page was not folded. It has no creases."

Nicki stared at the paper, then laughed. "That's the paper from Corrin's locker."

"So?"

"Think, Kim. Do that trick of yours and remember exactly what Corrin told Mr. Cardoza the day her paper was stolen."

Kim closed her eyes. A moment later she spoke in Corrin's voice: "I stopped by my locker to pick up my research paper. I worked *so hard* on it, Mr. Cardoza. But I couldn't find it, so I took all my books out and then I found this!"

Nicki elbowed Kim. "What else did she say?"

Kim's brow wrinkled in concentration. "I left my locker open for about ten minutes this morning so Heather could pick up a book I borrowed. Someone must have taken my report then. I didn't notice anything until just now. My report is gone and this was on top of my books!"

Nicki giggled. "Don't you see? Corrin was lying! One minute she said the *unfolded* paper was the *last* thing she found, and the next minute she said it was on top of her books—as if someone had folded it and slipped it in through the vent." Nicki stood and looked for the others. "Unless someone knew Corrin's locker combination, there's no way this paper could have been in her locker unless *she* put it there herself."

"But we must know for sure," Kim said. "We must have proof."

"You're right," Nicki answered. "So let's find it."

Nicki walked over to the lockers and gingerly touched the mystery mark painted on Corrin's locker. These figures weren't as tiny or detailed as the ones on the yellow paper, but anyone could tell what they were.

But what were they? Did the mark mean anything at all? She looked at Kim. "Are you sure these figures aren't Korean?"

Kim nodded. "Some Chinese figures are similar to Korean letters, but these are not."

Nicki tapped her fingers on the locker. "Okay. So if they're not Korean, maybe they are Chinese . . ."

"Hey!" An angry voice cut into her thoughts. "What are you doing with Corrin's locker?"

Heather walked up with Julie by her side. Nicki groaned. She did not need a visit from the Corrin Burns Fan Club right now.

"I'm not doing anything." Nicki shifted her books in her arms. "I only wanted to get another look at that paint job."

Julie snorted. "Planning to paint something else, huh? Well, don't touch my locker!"

"Why don't you find another cute guy and paint his?" Heather said, laughing. "That's why you do it, isn't it? So you can run over and bat your eyes and promise *you'll* solve the mysterious crime?"

"I've never painted anybody's locker," Nicki said. "I don't even know what that symbol means." She looked at the girls. "Do you?"

Heather snorted. "Corrin says it looks like sixteenth notes."

Nicki lifted a brow. "I didn't know Corrin was musical. She's not in the band, is she?"

Julie laughed. "Shows how much you know. Corrin has

played the harp for six years. Last year she won an award for a harp composition?"

Nicki looked at Kim. "She's a composer? That's cool." She grinned at Heather. "By the way, I'd like to borrow the book you loaned to Corrin."

Heather looked puzzled. "What book is that?"

"Remember? The day she left her locker open for you to pick up your book. The day her English paper was stolen."

Heather laughed, but some of the sizzle had gone out of her smile. "Oh yeah. Well, you can't borrow that book."

"Why not?"

"It's out of circulation."

Kim bowed slightly to the other girls. "Corrin got an A on her English paper, yes? It must have been a very good paper."

Julie and Heather looked at each other. "Of course it was good," Julie said. "She read the CliffsNotes instead of Shakespeare and changed the story into her own words. Her mother typed it."

Nicki shook her head. "How intelligent is that?"

Heather completely missed the sarcasm in Nicki's voice. "Oh yeah. Corrin is smarter than you think."

—

Nicki looked at Kim. "I've got to do something," she said, "and you need to go be with Laura and the others. It's a special day for your family and I don't want you to miss a minute of the festival."

Kim shook her head, but Nicki gently pushed her away. "If

the sun shines on the garden of my friend, I feel warm," she said. "I'll be happy seeing you up there with the others. Come on, Kim, I'll walk you to Mrs. Balian's room."

Laura, Meredith, Christine, and Mrs. Balian greeted Nicki and Kim with smiles. "We're meeting Scott and Mr. Padgett in the parking lot to take pictures around the limo, then Mr. Padgett's taking us to dinner," Christine said. "Nicki, we sure wish you could come, too."

"That's okay," Nicki said, not wanting to admit how much she missed being with them. "I'm working on something . . . I think it's important."

"I really wish you were going with us," Laura whispered. "I'm still worried, Nicki. I'm not quite sure there isn't something to this curse business. I haven't felt good all day."

"Probably just nerves," Mrs. Balian said, putting her arm around Laura's shoulder. "And now we have to get going if we're going to get you back here in time to change and ride over to the fairgrounds for the crowning of our queen." Something in the woman's smile made Nicki wonder if she really had been a runner-up in the Miss America pageant.

"I've got to run, too," Nicki said, and before her friends could protest, she hurried out the door.

# Seventeen

Nicki had never covered the mile between her home and school so quickly. Fortunately, her father was home and working at his big desk in the den. Theirs was the only home she knew of with two fully functioning offices.

Mr. Holland raised a finger to let Nicki know he'd be off the phone in a moment. "That will be fine," he said, smiling. "I'll be happy to meet with you next Thursday. See you then."

He hung up the phone and looked at his daughter. "What's up, Nicki-roo?"

Nicki grinned. Her father came up with the strangest nicknames for people.

"I need a favor, Dad. Actually," she said, sitting down on the edge of his desk, "it's a favor for Laura. She's afraid she has been cursed and she's really worried about being crowned queen at the Fall Festival."

"Laura Cushman? The girl who lost her father last year?"

"Right. Laura got a threatening note and she's scared someone's going to try to do something to her tonight. I was supposed to stick around and help her, but there's somewhere else I need to be." Nicki hugged her arms. "Could you stand in the crowd near Laura and make sure no one throws a pie in her face or anything like that?"

Mr. Holland laughed. "When you flash that dimple, kiddo, you know I can't say no. I'll have Josh and Sarah with me, though. Mom is supposed to join us after she shows a house at six-thirty, but I'll probably have my hands full till then."

"That's okay, Dad." Nicki knew how active her little brother and sister could be. "Just stand in the front of the crowd and keep an eye out—you know, like a Secret Service man or something. They're supposed to crown the king and queen at seven o'clock."

Mr. Holland nodded. "I'll defend her from enemies, foreign and domestic, at peril of my life and limb. I promise."

Nicki rolled her eyes. "Just don't let anyone trip her or throw mud in her face."

—

A blanket of quiet lay over the school when Nicki slipped through the large double doors at five-thirty. She padded down the wide halls toward Mrs. Balian's room, wincing once when her sneakers made a loud squeak as she crossed the tile floor.

If she had timed it right, Laura and the girls would be halfway through supper. Soon they'd be coming back here to change clothes and drive to the fairgrounds. While Mr. Holland guarded Laura from mischief at the fair, Nicki had a task to perform at the school.

What would the culprit do to Laura Cushman? Was that note intended only to scare her? Nicki had thought about it all afternoon. So far, the culprit had stolen three times—two reports and a dog, even though the dog was returned a day later. Apparently McArthur was even too much for the mystery person to handle. And how did the culprit explain the dog to his or her parents?

Nicki didn't think the instigator would physically hurt Laura—too many people around to do that. Stealing, vandalism, and mischief seemed more likely.

The door to Mrs. Balian's room was unlocked, so Nicki slipped inside and felt her way through the darkness of the windowless room. The pane of glass in the door had been papered over to give the girls privacy while dressing, and only a tiny bit of light filtered through the paper.

She walked to the tall closet on the side of the room and stepped in. She closed the door halfway and crouched in a comfortable position. Not a bad position to watch for anyone who might plan to sabotage Laura's coronation.

As her eyes adjusted to the dark, she was able to see a row of dresses hanging ghostlike against the opposite wall. Knowing her friends as she did, she could guess which dressed belonged to which girl.

Torrie Kelshaw's dark green taffeta hung closest to Mrs. Balian's desk, obviously intended tonight for Christine. A black knit dress with a silver drape looked as long and lean as Meredith, and a simple but elegant white gown with a black bow had to be the dress Mrs. Cushman had bought for Kim. Kim would love it—and she'd look great in it. The black satin bow would perfectly match her shiny hair.

A little apart from the others hung the most breathtaking dress

Nicki had ever seen. The material was a deep aqua, the identical color of Laura's eyes, and the bodice had been studded with beads and rhinestones. A full skirt completed the outfit, and on a desk Nicki could see a shoebox containing what looked like aqua heels. Laura really would look like a queen.

A sudden surge of self-pity swept over Nicki. She could be with her friends instead of hiding in a closet if not for . . . who? What? Why hadn't she been able to solve this mystery?

But there was no sense in moping now. Her mother would say it was too late to cry over spilled milk.

The door to Mrs. Balian's room clicked. Nicki drew in her breath as something fluttered in her stomach. Automatically, she reached out to draw the closet door a few more inches toward her.

Someone slipped into the room. Nicki held her breath as the intruder moved quietly through the rows of desks. Finally the shadowed figure stood in front of the dresses.

Why didn't the trespasser move?

The truth hit Nicki like a fist—the mystery figure couldn't see. Like Nicki, this person was waiting for his or her eyes to adjust to the dark.

Nicki pushed the closet door open. The stranger didn't move, but Nicki could see that the person was small, dressed in black, and holding something in her right hand.

Nicki slipped out of the closet as the culprit moved toward Laura's dress. Her hands came together as Nicki called, "Stop!"

The interloper jumped, then threw whatever she was holing

over her head. Nicki hurried toward the door and flicked on the light switch.

Corrin stood in the corner, wearing a beautiful black skirt and a black silk blouse. Nicki looked around and found the object Corrin had thrown.

"A bottle of India ink?" She reached for the bottle. "Why, you were going to pour this over Laura's dress!"

Corrin didn't answer, and as Nicki picked up the bottle, she realized Corrin had loosened the cap. Ink was now running over Nicki's fingers.

"Gross." Nicki sighed. "This stuff is murder to clean." She looked at Corrin. "I know you did everything, Corrin. I suspected it earlier, but now I have proof. You didn't have your paper ready when it was due, so you made up that story about a curse and the mystery mark. You enjoyed the attention so much you kept the story up for a while, didn't you?"

"Oh yeah?" Corrin flung her brown hair out of her eyes. "You're the one with ink all over your hands, Nicki Holland. I can tell the others that I found *you* here about to ruin these dresses. You couldn't handle being left out."

The door clicked again, and this time Mrs. Balian entered, followed by Laura, Kim, Meredith, and Christine. "Look!" Corrin pointed to Nicki. "I came in to wish you all good luck, and I found Nicki here with India ink. She was going to ruin everything for all of you! Look at her hands!"

Laura's eyes went wide. "Nicki Holland," she whispered. "I can't believe it!"

# Eighteen

Nicki couldn't believe what she was hearing. "Laura, you don't honestly believe that story, do you?"

Laura looked like she was about to cry. "I'm so nervous and upset I don't know what to believe."

Mrs. Balian reached for a paper towel in her desk drawer. "I'm glad I have these," she said. "You never know when an emergency is going to come up." She took the leaking bottle of ink and tossed it into the garbage can, then she turned to Nicki and Corrin. "Now, girls, someone had better do some explaining."

Corrin began to sputter. "I came in here to congratulate Laura. I'm first runner-up, after all, and I thought I should say something to show there were no hard feelings. But when I turned on the light, there stood Nicki Holland with that bottle of ink. She was ready to throw ink on those dresses!"

Mrs. Balian lifted a brow. "Then why were you near the dresses and Nicki nearer the door when we came in? Seems like you two should have been in opposite positions."

Corrin lifted her hand. "Um, I wasn't finished. When I saw what she was about to do, I ran over here to stand in front of the dresses. Then Nicki got scared, I guess, and started to run out the door, but you all came in."

"I see." Mrs. Balian motioned for Meredith, Christine, Laura, and Kim to sit down. "Laura, do you believe Corrin was coming here to congratulate you?"

116

Fire blazed in Meredith's eyes. "The Atlantic Ocean would freeze over first."

Mrs. Balian shook her head. "I was talking to Laura."

Laura managed a trembling smile. "I'd like to hear Nicki's story. She's been my friend for months and she's never once lied to me."

Mrs. Balian looked at Nicki. "Your turn."

Nicki took a deep breath. "It all began the day Corrin didn't have her English paper done. She told Mr. Cardoza that someone had stolen it from her locker."

Mrs. Balian made a face. "How could someone steal a report from a locker? Wasn't it locked?"

"She had Heather Linton and Julie Anderson say that Corrin had left her locker open for ten minutes. They knew she hadn't done her report. But they didn't know that later she planted the yellow paper with the mystery mark. She did that because she didn't like Kim Park."

"Lots of people found those yellow papers," Corrin said, sitting down at a desk. "Why do you think I'd put a paper in my own locker?"

"Because you wanted attention," Nicki said, walking to the closet where she had left her book bag. "You thought being 'cursed' would make someone like Scott Spence notice you more."

"Oh, we all noticed you," Meredith said, laughing. "The way you carried on was too much!"

Nicki pulled out her notebook. "Here are the four papers. The one that said DOG MEAT was found in Scott's locker. You were still trying to frame Kim, and you heard that Scott thought Kim was cute. Well, Kim is cute, but why should that bother you? Are you *afraid* of someone a little different?"

Corrin didn't answer, so Nicki continued. "You ruined Scott's report and tried to convince him that Kim did it so he'd stay away from her."

Corrin glared at Nicki. "That's nuts."

Kim spoke up. "No, it makes sense. Nicki mentioned in her geography report that dogs are sometimes used for food in Korea. It was that afternoon Scott's locker was painted and he found this note. At the same time, I heard someone in the girls' water closet—excuse me, rest room—whisper something about having paint on her fingers. We knew that whoever painted the lockers with the mystery mark had to be a girl."

Nicki picked up the story. "Scott's dog, McArthur, was taken on Saturday, but came home Sunday morning. Corrin lives in Scott's neighborhood and could easily have opened the gate and led him to her house that morning. Scott said the dog was so friendly, he'd go with anyone. But he eats so much that Corrin couldn't keep him very long. She turned him out of her yard on Sunday, but not before she put a yellow kerchief around his neck to keep the story of the 'curse' alive. Mack went straight home."

Christine shook her head. "Now it seems so obvious," she said. "But what about Meredith's curse?"

Nicki pulled another yellow paper from her notebook. "This page was the paper Meredith found in her book bag when Corrin stole her research paper on Shakespeare."

"Now, why would I do that?" Corrin demanded. "I handed in my own paper on Shakespeare and I got an A. I didn't copy Meredith!"

"Of course not." Nicki smiled. "That would be too obvious, since no one in this school talks or even *thinks* quite like Meredith. But you desperately needed an A and you knew you couldn't get one by yourself. So you got your information from CliffsNotes, and to make sure your paper wouldn't look bad next to Meredith's, you took hers and left this yellow paper so everyone would think the mysterious curse was alive and well."

"I did manage to turn in a paper," Meredith told Mrs. Balian, "but I had to write it from memory, and it wasn't typed like the original. I got the first B of my life on it."

"Why would Corrin suddenly care so much about her grades?" Christine asked. "I've known her since sixth grade and she's never cared about school—about the learning part, anyway."

Meredith snapped her fingers. "Being the queen of the Fall Festival has never been open to Corrin before this. And from the five most popular girls in school, the queen is the one who has the highest grade point average. Corrin wouldn't have made first runner-up without that A in English."

"That makes sense," Christine said, looking at Corrin.

"When you found out that I told Mr. Padgett we suspected Michelle, you teamed up with her to frame me, didn't you?" Nicki asked. "You unearthed Meredith's report as evidence against me. What Michelle didn't know, though, is that you're the one who stashed the ink in her locker."

Corrin turned her face away.

"This page," Nicki said, pulling out the yellow paper marked for Laura, "was a simple warning for Laura not to come to the fair tonight. If Laura had been too frightened to show up, Corrin would have been crowned queen—because she was the first runner-up."

"She'd be up there with Scott Spence," Christine said. "No wonder she was willing to go so far."

Laura's eyes widened. "Now I understand. When I decided to go through with the ceremony, Corrin showed up here to ruin my dress. She knew I'd never go up on that platform in a ruined dress, and there wouldn't be time to bring another out-fit from home."

"Just look at Corrin." Meredith pointed to the girl in black. "She's all dressed up. Why would you dress like that to go to a fair?"

Corrin blushed. "Of course I dressed up tonight. As first run-ner-up, I thought maybe I'd have to do something on the plat-form. Plus, I'm singing in the choir."

Nicki shook her head. "You and I weren't supposed to

even go to the fair tonight. Mr. Padgett told us to stay away from Laura."

"Then what are you doing here?" Corrin glared at Nicki and stood. "You haven't proven anything, Nicki Holland, so I'm leaving."

Mrs. Balian moved to block the door. "Hold on a minute, Corrin. I don't think Nicki is finished."

Corrin sank back into her chair, a worried look on her face.

Nicki held up the remaining sheet of yellow paper. "This paper has been through a lot. Corrin found it in her locker when her report was stolen, right?"

Corrin's lower lip had jutted forward in a pout, but she nodded.

"I splashed it with water once to make sure this black writing was done in India ink, which it was. Though this page has been wet and has been riding around in my notebook for weeks, you can still see that it has never been folded."

Nicki handed the page to Mrs. Balian. "Corrin had to put this paper into her locker herself because anyone else would have had to fold it to slip it through the locker vent. Corrin couldn't say the paper was left in her locker when her report was stolen because Heather had said she hadn't seen the yellow paper when she supposedly went to Corrin's locker. I guess Corrin didn't fill Heather in on the details of her plan."

"I feel so stupid," Meredith muttered. "That clue was in front of us the entire time."

Nicki nodded. "Heather and Julie knew Corrin hadn't done her paper, but they didn't know she was planning to invent the mystery mark and blame everything on Kim. She couldn't even trust her best friends with that secret."

Corrin put her head down on the desk.

"Corrin also knows about India ink because she's a musician," Nicki added. "She won an award for a harp composition—which means she knows about writing music with ink."

"Why, Corrin!" Mrs. Balian smiled. "I didn't know you were so talented."

When Corrin lifted her head, Nicki was surprised to see that her eyes were filled with tears. "No one can know that I play a stupid harp," she muttered. "It's not cool to come to school with a harp on your back, for pete's sake."

Mrs. Balian stepped forward and placed her hand on Corrin's shoulder. "You don't have to worry about what people will think of you," she said. "It takes all kinds of people to live in the world. We should appreciate our differences. I think you're fortunate to be able to play the harp."

Corrin folded her arms and Nicki could see that her chin was quivering. Kim stood, then walked forward and knelt by Corrin's desk. "I do not hate you," she said, "just because you play the harp."

Nicki looked at her teacher. "That's about it. There's only one thing we haven't been able to figure out."

Kim nodded. "The meaning of the painted letters," she said, standing. "The writing is not Korean."

Corrin sniffed and wiped a tear from her cheek. "I don't know what it means, either. I saw it on some frozen Chinese vegetables my mother was cooking. It was easy to remember because it looked like sixteenth notes."

Mrs. Balian moved toward her desk. "This will have to be settled later, but I think Nicki has done a convincing job of tying up the loose ends. I think you have some apologies to make, Corrin, plus some lockers to repaint. And Mr. Cardoza will have to adjust a couple of grades on a certain English paper."

Corrin looked at Meredith. "I still have your report. It's a little wrinkled, but it's readable. You can give it to Mr. Cardoza."

Meredith smiled in relief. "Whew. I won't have a B on my record anymore."

Christine giggled. "I wish I had a B. I got a C on my cockatiel paper."

Mrs. Balian checked her watch. "We're running out of time. Corrin, outside you'll find Mr. Padgett waiting with the limo driver. I want you to go and tell him the truth of what happened. Laura, you and the other girls have got to get dressed now or we'll be late." She winked at Laura. "We don't want to keep the king waiting, do we?"

They all laughed. Meredith, Christine, and Kim stood to get dressed.

Laura sat by Nicki. "I don't know what to say," she said, lowering her gaze. "For a minute there, I didn't know what was going on. I was confused, and I'm sorry I doubted you even for a minute."

Nicki gave her friend a wide smile. "It's okay. Things did get confusing for a while. But I'm your friend and you can trust me." She laughed and mimicked Laura's southern drawl. "Ah promise."

# Nineteen

Standing with her family in the crowd, Nicki watched as Laura Cushman was crowned seventh-grade queen of the Pine Grove Middle School Fall Festival. Kim, Christine, and Meredith stood behind her, smiling, and Scott Spence stood next to Laura and tried to act as though the crown on his head was no big deal. But when he caught Nicki's eye, he grinned.

Wow.

Mr. Holland saw that grin. "Who is that young man?" he asked Nicki. A teasing light gleamed in his eye. "Is he the one who might throw a pie in Laura's face?"

Nicki landed a soft punch on her father's arm. "He's a friend, Dad. And you don't have to worry about Laura anymore."

Mrs. Holland glanced over at her daughter. "Honey, why aren't you up there with your friends?"

"Long story, Mom," Nicki answered. "I'll tell you later."

Mr. Padgett called Mr. and Mrs. Sang Soo Park to the platform and introduced them to the crowd. "Our newest student comes from farthest away," he said, pulling a reluctant Kim to the front of the platform. "But Kim has made remarkable progress learning our language and making new friends."

The principal smiled at Kim. "Would you like to say anything?"

Nicki was sure Kim wouldn't say anything, but though the girl blushed, she took the microphone. "I would like to thank the students and teachers of Pine Grove Middle School for this night," she said in her soft voice. "But most of all I would like to thank Nicki Holland, who wanted to help my family. She also wanted to be my friend."

Mr. Padgett searched the crowd. "Nicki, would you come up here?"

Nick felt uncomfortable in her blue jeans when everyone else was dressed up, but she climbed the platform steps and stood next to Kim.

"As principal, I've learned to solve problems one at a time," Mr. Padgett told the crowd, "but Nicki and her friends have solved more than one problem today. Nicki, would you like to give this check to Mr. and Mrs. Park?"

Nicki took the check the principal handed her. "Mr. and Mrs. Park, we'd like to give you this check for . . . wow! Ten thousand dollars!" She grinned. "It's to help cover the expenses for your wife's operation," she explained as she handedthe document to Mr. Park. He bowed, and Nicki and Mr. Padgett bowed in return. Then Mr. Park turned and bowed to Laura, Scott, and the girls, and they bowed back. When Mr. Park bowed toward the audience, Nicki saw her dad bowing, too.

She skipped down the steps and took her father's arm. "That's enough, Dad," she said, laughing. "Later I'll introduce you to Mr. Park and you can shake his hand."

But when the ceremony was finished, Nicki was surrounded by her friends, including Scott Spence and Jeff Jordan.

I wish you had been with us at dinner," Laura said. "It wasn't the same without you."

"That's okay," Nicki said, remembering how Scott had grinned at her. "Being in the audience wasn't bad. You all looked great!"

Christine shifted in her fancy shoes. "Let's go *do* something," she said. "My feet are killing me and I'm hungry."

"Again?" Nicki couldn't believe Christine's appetite. The girl was always hungry.

"She was too nervous to eat at dinner," Meredith explained as they began to walk down a line of booths. "They served spaghetti and Chris didn't want to slurp it in front of Mr. Padgett."

"How about an egg roll," Nicki suggested, spotting a Chinese food vendor among the booths. "I didn't get any supper and I'm starving."

The group placed their orders and were waiting patiently when Scott nudged Nicki's shoulder. "Look." He pointed to a sign overhead. "It's the mystery mark!"

The girls stepped forward for a better look. The cook, an Asian man behind the counter, saw them looking up and walked toward them.

"May I help you?" he asked. "I am Larry Cho. Is something wrong with my sign?"

"Mr. Cho," Christine said, pointing upward, "what does that sign mean?"

"The third symbol," Meredith added.

Mr. Cho looked up, then nodded. "Ah yes. Roughly translated, the sign says, 'Better is a meal with friends than a meal with kings.' The third symbol is *peng*, the Chinese word for friendship."

Laura turned toward her friends and smiled. "Amazing! All along, Corrin's curse meant nothing more than friendship."

Nicki grinned and raised her egg roll. "Even though there is royalty among us, here's to a meal with true friends—whether or not they are kings and queens."

# Enjoy all of the
# Nicki Holland Mysteries

# The Case of the Phantom Friend

Can Nicki and her friends solve the mystery
with only one clue?

*A man's angry voice echoed in the house and reached the girls out-
side. "You're a foolish, silly old woman!" the man yelled. "And one
of these days you'll realize how wrong you are to oppose me. Just
you wait, old lady. You'll be sorry!"*

Nicki, Laura, Christine, Meredith, and Kim have found a
new friend in Lela Greaves. But someone has threatened Ms.
Greaves and now she could lose everything she loves. The
girls have one clue that they hope will lead to something to
save Ms. Greaves—if only they can solve the mystery before
it's too late!

# The Case of the Teenage Terminator

Tommy's troubles could mean danger for
Nicki and her friends!

*With a burst of nervous energy, Nicki dove to the safety of the win-
dowless side of the shed. As the others glided into place beside her,
she put her finger across her lips and knelt to listen.*

*"It's too hot in here," a voice said.*

*"It's too hot everywhere tonight, after your brilliant move,"
another voice answered. "I hope you're not planning on hiding out
here until everyone calms down. You'll be here a week."*

Christine's brother Tommy is in trouble, but he doesn't seem
to realize it. Nicki, Meredith, Christine, Kim, and Laura take on
an investigation that pits them against a danger they've never
faced before—one that could lead to a life-or-death struggle.

# The Case of the Terrified Track Star

Who would threaten Pine Grove's track star?

*Nicki saw Jeremy give Meredith a puzzled look. But then there was no mistaking the snarling howl that erupted from Mr. Nichols' yard.*

*It was just like Jeremy's nightmare. Nicki turned and saw the gate on the tall wooden fence swing open. There was a flash of bristly fir and teeth and anger. Killer was loose, and his fangs were bared and gleaming.*

*He was streaking right toward Jeremy Newkirk!*

Pine Grove's track star Jeremy Newkirk has always been afraid of dogs, but now somebody is using that information to scare him out of Saturday's important race. Without Jeremy, Pine Grove will never win! Following a trail of mysterious letters and threatening phone calls, Nicki and her friends are in their own race against time to solve the mystery. Can the girls keep Jeremy's worst nightmare from coming true?

# The Case of the Counterfeit Cash

Nicki's life is in danger!

In the gathering darkness, Nicki and Christine swam quietly toward the Mary Celeste II. The water was as black as ink around them, and Nicki tried not to think of the living things that might be passing by her in the warm water.

They reached the stern of the boat where the overhead light on deck threw shadows in the water. Nicki lifted her face mask. "Are you going to climb up, or should I?"

Christine's mouth fell open and her eyes bugged. "Behind you," she squealed. "Look!"

Nicki whirled around. Behind her something was rising out of the water—something big and dark and sinister, with arms like a giant sea serpent!

Nicki Holland expected fun and sun in the summer before her eighth grade year—not mysterious strangers and counterfeit cash! Nicki, Meredith, Kim, Christine, and Laura are warned to leave the mystery alone. But when Nicki is threatened, she has to solve the mystery to save her own life!

# The Case of the Haunting of Lowell Lanes

There's no such things as ghosts . . .

*"Hurry," Laura urged Meredith. "This place is spooky when it's this quiet.*

*Meredith stood at the end of the lane, concentrating. Suddenly the few remaining lights flickered. A bright figure appeared from nowhere and seemed to float over the lanes until it hovered over lane thirteen.*

*"Ohmigoodness," Christine whispered. "This place really is haunted!"*

Nicki and her friends thought it would be fun to help Meredith's uncle at Lowell Lanes for the summer. But then the lights went out and strange things began to happen. Is Lowell Lanes really haunted? Can Nicki and her friends solve the mystery before Mr. Lowell is driven out of business?

# The Case of the Birthday Bracelet

A beautiful birthday present holds much
danger and mystery . . .

*Nicki tensed when a muffled sound from the other room caught
her attention. She couldn't see into the room where Krisha,
Christine, and Laura were sleeping, but she could hear the faint
sound of someone moving around in the darkness. Had someone
come in? Had they forgotten to lock the deadbolt on their door?*

*Nicki slipped silently off her bed and padded across the floor until
she was in the doorway. She stiffened as she heard a thump from the
closet. If the girls were in their beds, who was in the closet?*

*Something jerked on the edge of her gown, and Nicki clapped her
own hand across her mouth to smother her scream.*

Nicki and her friends thought they were taking a nice vaca-
tion trip to London, but strange things begin happening even
before the girls arrive at their hotel. And when Laura's diamond birthday bracelet disappears, the search leads Nicki and
her friends to more danger than they had bargained for!

# The Secret of Cravenhill Castle

A deadly treasure hunt puts Nicki and her
friends in grave danger . . .

*A shadow fell upon the group as if a huge hand had passed before
the sun. A rumble came spiraling down from the clouds overhead,
and the wailing of the wind brought goosebumps to Nicki's arms.
Nicki looked toward Meredith, who opened her mouth in a sound-
less scream and pointed to something behind Christine. Coming
straight toward them was a radiant ball of dancing light.*

*Without warning, the light ball darted into the leaves of a nearby
oak tree. Even the air seemed to hold its breath until the top of the
oak tree exploded in a shower of green leaves.*

Nicki and her friends are thrilled when they receive an invi-
tation to spend a few days at a 500-year-old Irish castle.
Shrouded in mystery and fairy legend, the castle is everything
they expect, and more! The girls must battle the sea, supersti-
tion, and their own fears as they undertake a dangerous search
for the legendary treasure of Cravenhill Castle.

# The Riddle of Baby Rosalind

Can Nicki and her friends solve the riddle in time?

*To whom it may concern,*
*Thank you for taking care of my baby, Rosalind. I hope you will forgive me for the unexpectedness of this situation, but I cannot give Rosalind the home she deserves. I hope you will see that she is well taken care of and loved. Please do not let anyone harm her. Tell her I loved her very much.*
*Thank you.*

Nicki and her friends expected a normal flight home from Ireland until Laura meets a woman in the airport and offers to watch her baby. When the woman fails to board the plane with the girls, Laura and Nicki find a note in the baby's diaper bag. Did the mother really abandon the child? Was the woman in the airport really the baby's mother, or was she the kidnapper? Nicki and her friends have only eight hours to find answers to their many questions about the baby in their care.

# About the Author

Angela Hunt lives in Florida with her husband Gary, their two children, and two mastiffs, dogs that are even bigger than McArthur. Her favorite color is periwinkle blue and she loves pizza. You can read more about her and her books at www.angelahuntbooks.com.